The *Lilibet Logs*

T0351674

The *Lilibet Logs*

Restoring a Classic Wooden Boat

JACK D. BECKER

SHERIDAN HOUSE

Published 2006 by
Sheridan House Inc.
145 Palisade Street
Dobbs Ferry, NY 10522
www.sheridanhouse.com

Library of Congress Cataloging-in-Publication Data

Becker, Jack.
    The Lilibet logs : restoring a classic wooden boat / Jack D. Becker.
      p. cm.
  ISBN 1-57409-238-3 (alk. paper)
  1. Lilibet (Yacht) 2. Yachts—Conservation and restoration. 3. Ships, Wooden—Conservation and restoration. 4. Becker, Jack. I. Title.

VM331.B34 2006
623.822'3—dc22
2006013884

Technical advisor: Peter H. Spectre
Editor: Janine Simon
Designer: Keata Brewer

ISBN 10: 1-57409-238-3
ISBN: 13: 978-1-57409-238-7
Printed in the United States of America

For Georgia, my best friend.
Without her abundant care, very hard and
good work, and endless support, this project,
as well as many others, would not be possible.

Contents

The *Lilibet Logs*

From a letter to the author by the former owner of LILIBET

"In Road Town Harbour where she was a shrimp by comparison to most of the other vessels the most telling phrase was what one American said to me when we were in the middle of doing some varnish work: 'Every day I walk past your yacht I think that she is the most beautiful vessel in the whole damn marina, and every day I think, thank God she is not mine!'"

Introduction

Sometimes you just have to make a "left turn decision." Left turns—if you don't already know—are what some folks call moments in life when for no immediately logical reason, you just veer suddenly and sharply to the left at a ninety-degree angle, giving yourself a completely different direction. I don't know why the same thing couldn't be said of a "right turn," except perhaps that on the face of it, a right turn is in fact a "right" turn—possibly meaning a correct turn—whereas a "left" turn automatically becomes at least the possibility of being a wrong turn, so there's implied risk involved.

Whatever the semantics of the thing are, a well-made left turn changes life a little—sometimes a lot. Illogical, impractical, and impulsive are words that more often than not are applied by the "turnees" (those affected by the move; also, I suppose, by the attorneys in some instances), while for the "turner" (the one doing the turning), there's always some totally compelling reason for initiating the tactic.

By way of scenic background one might say that Minnesota, which I presently call home, likes to think of itself as a land of quiet fortitude, so the classic left turn is un-usual here. While our global climate shifts, seemingly changing Minnesota's notorious winters into something less grim than history details, the old boys still like to remember when you went from November to March without ever once removing your woolen long johns for fear of winding up in the pneumonia ward over at Sacred Heart. This reliance on the stability of terrible Minnesota winters and the resulting need to hold tight—plus perchance just a smidgeon of old-world Northern European demographics—seem to have generated a sort of regional admiration for the status quo. Come to think of it, wasn't the expression "If it ain't broke, don't fix it" first heard skipping across a trail of frozen cow pies somewhere up there on a farm in pre-dawn Hibbing? In that light, one might conclude that change is often seen hereabouts as a misfortune better left to those loose-livers out there in California, where left turns and such are part of the culture. Hereabouts, true left turns, like moving—heaven forbid—from the suburbs to the city, or vice versa, or to another part of the country, or growing a beard, or shaving one off, or selling your condo and buying a land-barge to visit the scattered relations and living on the road . . . well now, that's something else. (Oh, there was of course, that in-cident with the wrestler/governor—kind of a statewide left turn, but nobody remembers much about that.)

The thing about left turns, of course, is that they tend to be thematic (my theme is boats), and they can surely become a way of life. One must beware the slightly addictive allure and gauge carefully the distance between left turns so they don't run the wheels off the road, as we say. I was therefore most particularly attentive to this principle when I made my latest and recent move to the left; I had waited a good ten years before I dared try it. I made my move on a Monday in early September when I sent my money off to the boat broker in Maryland whose demeanor on the phone resembled to a tee the worst pirate character ever seen in a very bad movie. In the flash of a bank funds transfer, the deal was cooked, and I owned a wonderful little yacht and of course the restoration project that came with it. What a delightful, purposeful, devilish feeling! This was the boat that had been haunting the edges of my conscious mind while I drove to and from work. The very one that I've been cruising the docks and the ads and the Internet for. It would be the perfect project at this time in my life—so say I.

For those nervous types who hate the left turn, I'll point out that this was my third classic, antique, old, fixer-upper wooden boat. While staying true to my theme, it had been a while, however, since the last, and I calculated the ground swell of nay saying that might reach my shores because this was no bass boat, but a lovely little ocean racer sailing sloop. Having been here twice before and survived to some extent at least, one should guess that I was pretty far past the point of misunderstanding the many ways to crash and burn on this kind of adventure. Even with motivation aplenty, hard work, and good intentions combined, there were no guarantees for success—and, of course, that's the magic.

I was, until now, a stinkpotter. That is what sailors call those who drive powerboats. It's probably the result of engines on the water billowing smoke and fumes in great blue clouds trailing behind on otherwise calm and peaceful days. Generally we're thought of as an ill-natured and unpredictable bunch. Loud, pushy, overweight, simple minded, careless, artless, and with very bad taste in clothing. I must admit to most of those things, although being an artist, I can't quite accept the artless part.

Stinkpotters refer to sailors as "ragbaggers," due of course to the mounds of bulging sail bags tied on every part of a sailboat. There's a tendency among powerboaters to think of sailors as skinny, snooty, pushy, elitist, and much too athletic (in fact, a friend once referred to sailboats as floating gymnasiums). Just to prove how special they are, sailors have invented a whole private language for things they do while sailing—such as "trim the stays'l (that's stay-sail) and reef the main; fall off, head up, hard a-lee, jibe-ho, sheets, vangs, downhauls, outhauls, heave-to, etc., etc.," all of which can make for a rather exclusive conversation around a dinner table.

Powerboaters tend to say things like "Let's drop the anchor, shall we?" or "We're out of beer. Let's head for the marina." I remember an embarrassing incident of running out of gas in the middle of the shipping lanes near the port of Seattle on our way home from a weekend of shrimp netting in the Hood Canal. My powerboating buddies, standing on the bow of my dead-in-the-water twin-engine stinkpot, made the following resolution: "When in doubt, EAT" and headed for the galley. Another stinkpotter friend dismissed the whole sailor "thing" by claiming those snooty ways are just because ragbaggers are envious of our powerboat generators and refrigerators and onboard laundry facilities and cushy furniture.

The actual dynamics of boat style choices, of course, may be uncovered in some future sociology graduate student's master's degree thesis, which sadly none of us will ever read, but any time spent on the water will attest to the wonderfully pointed differences between powerboat enthusiasts and sailors. (Thinking about it now, having several years of the following experience under my belt, some things about these differences do seem to make better sense. I'll save those revelations for later.) For now it might suffice to say that, North and South, East and West—there just is this funny disdain for each other's leisure lifestyle choices, and it makes for wonderful people watching.

While driving my powerboat, therefore, I always give sailboats a wide berth on the water because they generally have the right of way if they are sailing without engine power, plus I can never tell just what they're intending to do as they keep getting closer. There's a little game of "chicken" that goes on sometimes. Even with miles of water on both sides, no one wants to turn off their course, so tension builds. The guy in the powerboat is saying, "That dirty rotten sailor is going to cross right in front of me just to show that he has the right of way, and I'm going to have to shut down the mill and cram this thing to the right (that's starboard) fast, to avoid spilling the drinks." Sailor Joe is saying, "Look at that clod in the powerboat. Thinks he owns the ocean. I bet I've got enough wind, so I'll cross his bow and scare the crap out of him." Most times, the boats skid by each other and everyone exchanges dirty looks. The stinkpotters tend to be more vocal. They like to wave their fists around, sometimes with a middle finger sticking up. The ragbaggers tend to look calm and superior behind their flashy sunglasses.

We began our boating life in Seattle, Washington, where there are more boat owners per square foot around Puget Sound than anywhere in the country, except perhaps the Chesapeake Bay on the East Coast. We—my wife Georgia, our son Yascha, and I—had moved to Vashon Island (20 minutes to Seattle by ferry) from Minnesota, and our fiberglass Minniwawa canoe seemed slightly under scale for the big water, so I started hanging out at the docks. It didn't take long to discover some basic facts about this plethora of floating real estate.

(a) Old boats are cheaper than new ones; (b) most old boats are wooden construction; (c) most old boats need a lot of TLC (that's why they cost less); (d) many old boats are really beautifully designed and have the potential of cleaning up nicely; (e) Seattle has an abundance of old wooden boats for sale; (f) quite a few people are into owning and restoring old wooden boats, so you don't feel like the only fool on the beach; and (g) for some people, the smell of wood rot, fungus, and sawdust combined with paint fumes, varnish, and diesel fuel make the perfect antidote for what we in Minnesota call "cabin fever." Some of us have discovered that what comes along with that musty old derelict in distress is the feeling that there is a kind of life or soul to this pile of wood that needs your care. That feeling translates, of course, to gazillions of hours of your time. By the end of the first month, nobody asks where you are because there's only one answer to that question, and you've noticed a creeping leak in your bank account. Welcome to the club.

Because I was—and still am in many ways—a novice to the restoration process, and because I wanted to get right out there and go boating, I shied away from the gallant old hulls that reeked of rot and felt dead to the touch. After sticking my fingers through plenty of mushy wood and puddling through dark old saloons awash with oily salt water, I decided to look for something seaworthy. This decision was fortuitous in that it was a perfect entrée into the world of wooden boats and set me right in my future thinking when it came to the potential purchase of a project. The question being, how bad can bad be, without being so bad as to be too bad? This is the question we all must ask and know the answer to when we stand alongside our essential lover, hull down in ooze but still longing to swim.

At one of the marina docks on the ship canal in Seattle, I found a smart-looking old (1938) Matthews trunk-cabin cruiser. The BIG DIPPER—that was her name, and although I never liked the name, I loved the boat. Matthews is, or was, an Ohio boatbuilder with a great reputation. This boat had survived time because of some gentle ownership and good care. She was 40-foot-long, with twin Chrysler Crown gas engines, nice wood, good tight teak decks, and lots of shiny mahogany in the main saloon. She was my first real boat and, thankfully, required only simple tinkering and paint to make her suitable as a beautiful training boat for a young family. We kept her for five years, and besides using her as an exotic little weekend pad in the city where she was moored, we traveled around Puget Sound and into the San Juan Islands for great summer vacations.

BIG DIPPER taught us the rules of the road. She also taught us docking, anchoring out, chart reading, tide tables, and how not to behave in the various days-end marinas where we spent the night tied up. Big gangs of white yachts filled with mostly stinkpot revelers—sun burned and weary—formed great fleets in all the little harbors from Olympia, Washington, to Vancouver, British Columbia, and beyond. Kids and dogs and cats squirming along the decks, fat mommas barking out counter orders to the captains, semi-naked nymphs flashing tanned buttocks cruising the docks, glad to be free of confinement on the TUPPERWARE TIGER. As the sun goes low and the cockpits fill up with sea vacationers, chomping on Dungeness crab legs, trading stories, comparing this and that about each other's boat, charcoal smoke and barbecue smells drift along the water. Barrel-chested captains under straw hats stretch out in their deck chairs sucking up martinis, grateful for another safe day on the water, no contact with the office, no dreaded mechanical failures, and a harbor full of likewise folks.

Some summers and many boat stories later we left the island and moved aboard the great yacht DENALI. Talk about left turns. Our first boat was sold to a nice young banker lad who moved to Alaska and resold her to a young family from Issaquah, Washington. It was nice that she stayed a family yacht. Also nice that she didn't go to Alaska.

DENALI was an 85-foot commuter yacht built at Luders Marine Construction Company in Stamford, Connecticut, in 1926. She was Coast Guard-documented and said by many to have belonged to Al Capone when he was at his peak performance—although nothing on her documentation showed that ownership. The Luders yard burned down years later and when I called young Luders—the son—to ask about this boat, he did remember her (named AMIDA) but had no idea who had commissioned the building. The story goes that she was kept in Miami, Florida, at Al's big stucco joint on some canal, and Al spent a little time aboard when on vacation from being crime boss in Chicago. When Al went to prison, the boat was confiscated by the Feds, and when WWII broke out she joined a fleet of similar vessels to patrol the Southern coastal waters in case of attack from German U-boats. After the war, she was purchased by someone in California, brought around through the Panama Canal on her own bottom, and eventually sold to a couple from Seattle who took her to Alaska, where she lived for some time. Eventually needing quite a facelift, she was sold to a church camp in the San Juans and used to transport campers back and forth from the mainland.

We saw DENALI in the Duwamish Canal, tied to a dock and for sale. By now we were a family of four—add a 5-year-old daughter (Jordan), a boat girl from the start. We hauled DENALI at the Fisherman's Terminal in Seattle, repainted her bottom, replaced one short plank and moved aboard her with a baby grand piano, an Irish wolfhound (strange, but true), and an ornery Siamese cat, who would catch ducks at night and bring them only half murdered onto the boat. We lived on Lake Union in the middle of Seattle for four wonderful years. I took a skipper's class, and we chartered the boat for four-hour cruises around Lake Washington, doing wedding cruises, office parties, birthdays, and even some political fund-raisers. The piano got a workout, and we got pretty good at night driving.

These, however, are boat stories from the past, and as good as they seem to me, this bit of writing is just a foreword to the present. Now 15 years later, we are back in Minnesota after eleven years in Seattle and a nine-year side trip to Florida, where we owned no boats. So this is a log—or a record, starting date around August 10, 2002—of what might possibly be my dumbest, craziest, or perhaps my best boat project yet. Wish me luck.

Finding Lilibet
on the Internet

LILIBET is a sailboat. Actually she's a racing sailboat built of wood in England in 1937. Drawn by the noted British yacht designer Norman Dallimore for a Major Bill Noot, LILIBET is one of 58 yachts built to designs by Dallimore, whose boats are noted for their excellent construction and quality materials. Her hull is pitch pine over oak frames with copper fastenings. Her decks are teak sprung planking (meaning the deck planks follow the arc of the hull shape and tie into a nibbed king plank on either end of the boat), and she has a 55-foot-tall Sitka spruce mast. She measures 36 feet at the waterline and 42 feet on deck. She has been re-powered with a Perkins 4-cylinder 51-horsepower diesel, which has at this writing a recorded 250 hours of use. I'm not really sure of the actual engine hours past the paperwork received with the yacht broker's description.

In 1998 LILIBET sailed on her own bottom from England to Bermuda, lived in the islands for some years, and finally made her way to Chesapeake Bay where I found her. Actually, I found her on the Internet from my office in Wayzata, Minnesota. Don't ask me why I stopped at the picture of this boat because I don't know. She was priced

LILIBET, a classic ocean cruiser, fully restored

above my means, and she was a sailboat. As my brother said over the phone, "What the hell is that about?" I have no practical explanation so I won't even try.

Well, maybe just a little.

I'd been seriously looking at boat ads for some time. Most marinas in Minnesota are nothing like those on the Atlantic or Pacific coasts, which are loaded with boats of every description and price range, but what the heck, there is no ocean in Minnesota. Once in a while I would go on daylong car trips along the Mississippi River from St. Paul south, rummaging through all the marinas I could find. Slim pickings.

Newspaper boat ads in Minnesota consist mainly of Alumacraft fishing boats or small Chris-Craft fixer-uppers that the recently departed Uncle Rupert had been working on for the past seventeen years in his backyard—and of course one should figure this out pretty fast, we're a lake state. Oh sure, there's Lake Superior, the great inland sea, way up there four-plus hours away by car, and there's the Mississippi on our eastern border, but hang on there. Aren't we the land of ten thousand lakes? It says so on our license plates. True enough, but what they don't say in the travel brochures, is that we are really the land of nine thousand nine hundred little lakes and eighty largish lakes that are mostly shallow and twenty lakes big and deep enough to qualify for serious boating. Pretty much all of these twenty lakes are located so far off the beaten track that only those seeking isolation and mosquito squadrons can stand to be there.

I didn't exactly miss these facts when my thoughts switched from power to sail. In fact I made the required calls to various marinas. I checked the scene. Yes, it would be a little dicey, but there are some places that just might work. . . .

When some people call across the country about a yacht, things like a draft measurement of seven feet don't immediately register as danger signals. If I were a native-born Minnesotan, of course, I would have immediately registered alarm and switched to the pursuit of the classic Chris-Craft runabout. I, on the other hand, am a native son of Chicago. City of broad shoulders. Big guts, rolled up sleeves, cocked hats and stogies. Pig butcher to the nation, etc., etc. So what's the big deal about a seven-foot keel? Well, actually something registered in my brain about water depth in the Midwest, but who listens when there's a magic photo filled with all the boat things one desires looking out of the desktop screen?

Still, once things got serious, before I really did the deal—in fact between the time I took the trip to Annapolis where the boat was laying, made the offer, and then actually spent the money—I had to find a home for her, so I made the rounds of all the marinas and boatyards. I called the docks on Lake Minnetonka near my office first. It's a great big lake and has pretty good depth with a fair number of marinas. Two of them have sailboat moorage and Travelifts for hauling out. Wow! What if I could put this boat near where I work? I could stop by and putter for an hour or so on my way home at night. I could grin with pride as I rolled by on my way to work in the mornings.

Initial calls, however, were not encouraging. Probably deep enough water. Probably enough yard space for winter storage. Probably costly, but doable. Oops! You said wooden? How big? Sorry, we don't really have room for a boat that big. After several similar calls, I stopped to consider the situation. Without trying to be rude, it seems my office is located at a flashy little art center in the Twin City's most tony suburb. Everything here is—well—very special, including, it seems, the marinas.

Here's a bit of news that I might have sensed if I had kept up with my wooden boat chatroom gossip, or if I had been active in the boating community between the time I left Seattle until now. What used to be a perfectly natural item at most marinas—that is, a wooden boat or two, or even more—has in many places around the country become an unwelcome addition to the neighborhood. While the concept seems ludicrous—so that's why that gang of folks has been standing around for so long down on the riverbank, waiting all these years for fiberglass to get invented—well, you know where I'm going.

The thing is, wooden boats might spell trouble. Projects and dreams gone sour, sudden leaks and sinkings, old abandoned hulls left to rot. And then there's the woody folks themselves. Good-for-nothing dock-rat wooden boat owners loafing about, an unwelcome sight to the spotless world of fiberglass. Sods in old dungarees covered in paint and caulk slogging around the marina. Probably even pony tails. Oh no, can't have that!

This painting of everyone with the same brush is, of course, an unfair discrimination. As a rule, most wooden boat owners take a great deal of pride in keeping the old girl shipshape and spend countless hours in fair and foul weather keeping their boats looking right. Still, we all have seen how it can be, and I had to admit that in her present state, my new boat was nothing to brag about in the fine finish department.

One by one I visited all the boatyards around the lake. Some wouldn't even talk to me. Most claimed a short depth of water (your keel is too deep, Jack), not enough power in their Travelift (your boat is too heavy, Jack), some didn't like sailboats period, and of course the pretty unanimous "We don't take wooden boats" chorus wherever I went. All but one.

There is a little country yacht club and marina down the lake from my office that is owned by an old sailor who likes wooden boats. I stopped by to see him one day. Didn't flash any pictures of LILIBET in her current condition, and although we both agreed she was too big for the water here, I could see there was some interest. Especially when I said she was 42-foot-long, and he calculated the slip charges. I kept him in the ship's log for future reference.

Finally exhausting plan A, the lakes, I was left with plan B, the Mississippi River. It runs right through both Minneapolis and St. Paul. In Minneapolis, there isn't enough of a river to turn around in, plus there are the locks and bridges that interrupt everything. In St. Paul, though, a number of marinas dot the shoreline, and one of them has a yard full of the very things disallowed in the places I'd checked. Wooden boats. Let's call it Watchamajig Marina. That's a pet name I started using as I grew familiar with it. It is located at the bottom of a long hill that leads from the highway to the river bottom just west of downtown St. Paul and is distinctive in its rows of old woodys in various states of restoration—or disrepair, as you like. I had reconnoitered this place a time or two over the past couple of years and knew that some day I might find myself doing a project boat here.

As it turned out, Watchamajig Marina is also distinctive in its personality. As yards go, compared to what most of us imagine a marina to be, the place certainly has a character of its own. I bet some of this character comes from where it's located, because once you drive down the long, steep road leading from the city and find yourself in the trees at the bottom of those high limestone bluffs along the river there, you just about lose track of time and place. In summer, the boats live in a little pocket pond that has been dredged into the bank of the Mississippi. Other than the marina barns, there are no buildings or commercial development within sight—except for the haunted bat cave built into a natural cavern on the bluff side of the road across the street from the marina. A privately sponsored group does a Halloween spook thriller attraction for the public in October, and most of the outdoor decorations stay put throughout the year. There's always a gargoyle perched above the boarded up entrance, even in July. There really is nothing else around but wild river parkland and the marina. The bluffs also form a sound barrier, so except for the occasional jet plane arriving or departing at the Twin Cities terminal up river, it can be strangely silent.

Just outside the narrow water entry to the pond, brown old Mr. Mississippi just keeps rollin' along. It's not a big, broad expanse. The distance across is maybe 100 yards, and on the other side are more river bottom woodlands—thick with brush and seemingly impenetrable. Looking up river as well as down, you don't get any of those long, pretty, river valley views, because the marina is located on a bend in the stream that just doesn't allow for long-distance scenery, so the whole place is somewhat isolated. It's always a bit surprising to look up from a project just in time to see the passing of one of those steel barge leviathans shoved along by a big pushboat. Scary to think of being out on the river avoiding contact.

Back on shore, long rows of un-launched boats sit side by side, covered in mostly blue plastic, much of it only half secured and flying around in the breeze. Hulks that have lived here for years litter the yard. Old cars poke their noses from between the tented hulls. Houseboats lay side by side both in and out of the water—some having year-round live-aboard residents (even in our subzero winters) who use the marina restrooms and laundry. Two big boat barns house the shops where, if you are a trusted long-term tenant, you may enter and perhaps receive a little help from one of the marina big shots. A local wooden boat guru works out of these barns, repairing and restoring boats. He is a good craftsman and not unfriendly, but it's plain to see that he keeps a little distance from guys who do their own work.

Generally, the place is a kind of little old river town microcosm movie set. As it turned out, it was perfect for a big restoration project.

Somehow I wasn't surprised—and was actually relieved after my reception at the lake—to find a fairly optimistic attitude about bringing LILIBET to the yard. Yes, they could launch a sailboat with seven feet of draft (that turned out to be slightly optimistic). Yes, they could step and rig a 55-foot wooden mast (that turned out to be wildly optimistic). Yes, I could work on her in the yard. The cost of storing her was incredibly cheap. Yes, the river was deep enough, so I could take her downstream to the only logical place for sailing: Lake Pepin, a 40-mile-long wide spot in the river (also optimistic). I had already made contact with the Lake City Marina, a municipal boat docks in Lake City, on Lake Pepin, and got myself on their five-year (that's right) waiting list. I'm number 162. I thought it best to get on that list some time ago, even if I didn't buy the boat. When I signed up I neglected to mention that I was a woody.

Annapolis —
Love at First Sight?

With the storage and project workplace problem solved, I returned to the immediate task of actually making this boat purchase happen. Recognizing the danger in too much early homework analysis—that is, inventing a million reasons why buying the boat is a dumb idea—I got back on the Internet and found the original ad. Still there, still way too pricey, but something about the appearance suggested further investigation, so I called the broker in Maryland.

"Oh yesss," he said, "the great yacht LILIBET. Well now, she's had some hard use, but she was built right in the beginning and she's still in great shape. The lads who own her brought her up from the islands and went back home to England. She needs a new home. What's that? Taking on water? Oh no. Tight as a drum. Solid as a rock. Straight as an arrow. She does need some work though."

"How much will they take for her?" I asked in my best business voice.

We all know, by the way—and if you don't, I know you'll forgive me—that it is extremely bad form to freely, without a good deal of wheedling and a little firewater to loosen the tongue, quote boat prices on restoration projects until after you've made that rare and lucky killing by finding one of the two other people in the world who share your passion for this old boat and can afford to indulge, so I won't. The situation being that even if you paid just two dollars for the old girl, your friends and family in the peanut gallery would all say you got royally screwed. Not a good start to an admittedly challenging project.

And then, of course, next, without fail, comes the second big question: " Well, how much you gonna sell it for when yer done?"

I always answer by saying something like, "Gosh Harvey, I don't know." Then I love to watch the glaze frost over Harvey's eyeballs, because I can hear the wheels turning in his cerebral calculator. Sometimes I wonder if this profit calculating thing might come from too much exposure to television shows like Antiques Road Kills, where trash from a garage sale turns out to have astounding value. Maybe, but I'm guessing there's probably more to it than that, and this is an important element in the whole joy of impracticality attached to restoration projects like LILIBET. It's the work-to-value thing. So feature this, if you will. In this place of quiet fortitude and sketchy crop prices, bad winters and dead batteries, here in the heartland, there isn't a lot of room for impracticality. Harvey believes that if you're going to buy this outrageous piece of crap, and spend time and money fixing it up, there must be some underlying profit motivation that drives the project. Sorry, Harvey. I know you won't understand this, and I'll never expect you to, but this is pretty much just a lot of work for the pleasure of working.

With this in mind, and with the ever-present threat of the exchequer over my shoulder, I listened carefully for the answer to my question, "How much will they take for her?" Long John was quick on the draw and fired back a number. It was half the price quoted on the Internet, and it made me curious. I probed a little and thought I detected just the whisper of that boatman's illness called "Don't want her." Especially when he said, "Minnesota? Oh yes, that's a great spot for her."

I needed a trip anyway and hadn't been east in a long time, so I booked a weekend flight to Baltimore and a room in an Annapolis B&B.

If you ever get to feeling boaty, that is, in need of buying a boat, but are not terribly sure about it and want to do something that pushes you over the edge of reason and into the lap of acceptance, I recommend a weekend by yourself in Annapolis. Georgia had recognized the signs and made plans to visit her parents. "You'd better go alone," she said. I did. I got there late on Friday night after a long pitch-black drive from the Baltimore airport.

Old Annapolis is a gaggle of narrow, angled cobblestone streets, all sort of radiating out from the central harbor, and it took me a while to locate my inn along the dark side streets next to the Naval Academy. I found the keys to my room in an incredibly quaint old residence under the outside doormat and set off down the cobbled streets for a whiff of the night air before turning in.

This was in early September. The air was crisp, and the

trees were already orange and yellow. Leaves had begun to gather on the walks and yards, and inside the narrow colonial-style houses things looked warm and cheery. Sometime after midnight I made my way back to the inn and in a great state of excitement crawled under the big, fluffy comforter on the old bed in my room and passed out. In the morning I browsed around the family-style breakfast table, listening to the chatter from my fellow guests who were in town for a wedding. Hardly able to concentrate on civil conversation, I excused myself, wished them all a great wedding day, and drove down the coast along the Chesapeake to a weather-worn little marina on one of the many river outlets along the bay. I spotted a tall, varnished wooden mast amongst the aluminum ones as I drove in and guessed rightly that it was on the boat I had come to see.

LILIBET at the dock in Maryland on the days of Jack's first visit, Fall 2002

The salesman I had been in contact with turned out to be every bit the Long John Silver type I had imagined, except he had both legs; we set off down the docks. I gathered images as we got closer.

LILIBET's hull above water is quite delicate as are all the old racers. She has a long, tapered transom that starts from the boottop—the painted stripe that defines the waterline—just about below the center of the cockpit and runs up and back to the stern, forming a classic cantilever over the water. Her bow leans forward in a nice little curve that Long John termed a knuckle bow. She has a long trunk cabin that meets a raised doghouse forward of the cockpit.

My first impression was that of looking at a hard-used and very tired sailboat. She was dirty and unkempt, lines lying about the decks as though someone had just brought her in from a cruise. Her paint was literally peeling off the hull; the old wooden cheek blocks on her rigging were cracked; the iron hardware was badly rusted and in some cases falling apart; the bronze parts were clogged with green corrosion from the sea salt. The sail covers were threadbare, tattered, and barely able to hang on; the dodger looked as if it had been fried by the sun; the brightwork was badly weathered. Faded sail bags cluttered the cabin topside. Long John chatted away about the great history of this boat, his own sailing experience, the great potential of restoration, the weather. He was a large and elderly guy, so hopping aboard from the rickety dock finger where LILIBET was tied became something of an event. I'm a large and elderly guy, too, and I was pleased to find it much less of an event for me.

It's difficult to say what turns one on when it comes to choosing a boat. With DENALI it was the covered walk-arounds alongside the main saloon and the vast forward deck. With the BIG DIPPER, it was her low-slung silhouette. Something quite impractical is what usually gets you going. A friend in Seattle found a boat in San Francisco that was truly everything he dreamed of, but what really got him reaching for his checkbook was that amazing bit of wood-work that brought the stairway curving down into the main saloon from above decks.

Nothing in particular about LILIBET grabbed me. The best I can say is that in my life I have owned two British go-machines. One was a 1953 MG TD. It was my very first au-tomobile and a mechanical terror. Nothing about it had an ounce of practicality, as my parents were eager to point out. It flapped and vibrated down the road at a top speed of fifty miles per hour. It leaked oil. (No disrespect meant for our allies, but the British, I learned from experience, never seemed to quite master the making and fitting of gaskets). It always had some little widget out of whack, and I was forever duct-taping and wiring things in place. But my God, was it ever cool. Those long, low shovel fenders swooping up from the running boards, topped with big chrome headlights. Those side doors that opened the wrong way. That square chrome grill and rectangular engine bon-net with louvers all along the sides. That abbreviated rear end with the outside gas tank. The green leather interior. Those wing nuts everywhere. Well, it was just my car.

My second British go-machine was a Triumph motorcycle. Also long and lean, customized into some kind of maverick chopper with an extended front fork and straight pipes (no mufflers), so loud it rattled your teeth. Of course it leaked oil all the time.

Perhaps this doesn't relate exactly to my sudden attraction to the little English racing yacht under my feet, but in many ways there was a familiar feeling as I enjoyed the moment.

Long John meanwhile was opening the cabin doors. His sudden burst of cursing brought me back to the present, and I peeked over his shoulder into the cabin. The warm smell of diesel fumes and battery acid and wet wood brought back old times, but the sight of brown water sloshing above the cabin sole really got my attention. The boat was indeed taking on water. So much for the "tight as a drum" part of this deal. Amidst a flurry of expletives and apologies, and a dangerous leap back onto the rickety dock finger, Long John thumped off down the dock to get a pump—the batteries on board were, of course, dead. It gave me a chance to survey the dark interior.

We must remember here that this was totally uncharted territory for me. 'Till now, my experience on sailing vessels amounted to sitting on some cockpit bench perhaps three times as a guest, while the owner and his crew—usually one other person—hauled on some line or another in very flat water and we moved along on our way to dinner at a restaurant. As a stinkpot skipper, I always considered existence below the waterline an extremely unusual way to have a good time, and just the gloom alone of most sailboat interiors put me off in a big way.

Now, here I found myself balanced on a pile of soggy life vests in the middle of a very flooded, dark, cramped, and smelly cabin, taking stock of the mess before me. For a moment, I could do nothing but stare in disbelief. Unnerving as the presence of the oily flood on the floor was, the rest of the interior reflected as bad or worse conditions. It looked as though whoever sailed this boat up from the south had done everything possible to trash the interior. Hard to take it all in, but the glaring feature overall was the total disregard for comfort designed into the inside of this boat.

The interior was sparse to the point of being prison-like. After being on a good many boats over the years, this one felt as depressing as the bottom of a well. Add to that a sort of general hodgepodge of parts. The instruments were scattered around the cabin, sort of tacked up here and there, wherever someone took a notion. No plan by the look of it. Most items looked like World War II surplus, with wires running every which way along and under the cabin tops and bulkheads. Every so often all these wires would come together into some sort of distribution box. Most of these connecting junctions had tails of disconnected wires sprouting like whiskers. The interior stank of diesel fuel in a bad way. The teapot was still on the stove top as though someone had gone out shopping and would soon be back. The stove sides ran with dried spillage from past cookery. Storm cloths hung in the closet. Damp books lined the meager

LILIBET's interior from the mast looking aft, when I first stepped aboard. You can see daylight reflecting off the standing water on the cabin sole and the soggy bed cushion on the left shelves. Maps and charts lay about as though recently consulted. No attempt to be clean or tidy could be seen, and I wondered who these guys were and how they survived the heat and humidity of the islands living in this way. Surprising the boat hadn't run onto a reef and sunk, with all the apparent disregard for conditions of health and welfare that showed here.

We rigged a pump and soon brown water was sloshing over the side and into the bay. Before long I could squish along the soaked floor carpet and explore the interior. The farther in I got the rougher it looked. Still, optimist that I am, within 15 minutes there I was listing in my head the order of things that had to be done. I asked for a little time to explore the boat by myself; I needed time to recover and think. John was only too glad to get off and back to his office. "No problem," he said.

When he was gone I tried to take in the full import of what this boat needed, and what I realistically could give to it. General labor I could supply by the bucket full. I'm pretty good with tools and have a fair amount of concentration when it comes to finishing projects. What gave me pause, however, was the whole library of unknown eccentricities peculiar to sailing vessels. Apart from taking note of the general decline of all the outside woodwork—and there was plenty of that—the more alarming part to me was my total ignorance of the workings of a sailing machine. I mean here were all sorts of ropes of many colors, sizes, braids, or wraps, some great, large wire cables, some thin and very rusted cables, and a great many of them coming down from the mast in all directions to hook to the boat by various turnbuckles, clamps, snap shackles, and whatever. The lifelines along both sides of the boat sagged loosely, and some of the old stanchions wobbled dangerously as I brushed past them.

The deck caulking was old and dry, and I could tell from the running stains on the inside cabin woodwork that the decks leaked severely. At some time she had run her bow pulpit into a dock or wall of some kind, because the topmost chrome loop, which sticks out over the bow, had a rakish slope not bent intentionally at the factory. I dithered as long as I could but finally decided to escape and clear my head. I stopped at the office and scheduled another meeting for the next day, then drove the three miles back to Annapolis for a long evening of scheming.

I remember sitting at a street-side fish restaurant trying to talk myself into a negative attitude, but it didn't work. Young salts-to-be from the Naval Academy walked by in their summer whites, and crowds of tourists hung along the concrete rim of the circular harbor, peering into the long line of beautiful yachts moored as guests for the night. Steaming crab cakes arrived at my table, as did a couple of cold Haakbecks. I watched the summer crowd, and I went back to thinking about the little yacht LILIBET.

In many ways, if one is looking for both a doable though daunting project and a wonderful challenge—I told myself—and can stand to expect a certainty of financial drain, this was exactly the right boat. In other ways, the whole idea of buying a derelict sailboat was just a bit ridiculous. In fact buying a sailboat at all seemed pretty amusing, too. Back and forth, back and forth, I went over the pros and cons, yet in the end the thing happened as I almost certainly knew it would. I liked the boat. So now, really, the only challenge was to decide what low number would do the deal. I had called a Wisconsin boat transporter the week before my trip to get a quote on trucking this thing from Annapolis to St. Paul. He had a one-way load going east to Havre de Grace, Maryland, so I could get a one-way charge west to the Twin Cities. Okay, that worked. I had the number of a boat surveyor in my pocket, but I would wait to see if my offer was accepted.

I spent part of the evening in a little flurry of tourist shopping through the cobblestone streets of Annapolis. It was crowded and lots of fun—especially when I rounded a corner and found the biggest boating supply store I had ever seen. Rows and rows of neat stuff for every boat of every kind. How strange to find myself looking at winch cranks and cheek blocks and lazyjack rigs instead of standup refrigerators and fancy drawer hardware and shower stall inserts as in the old days of powerboating. And how odd to admit that most of it seemed like something from under the hood of a foreign racing car: I had no idea what any of it was used for—except, well, "sailing." I spent the rest of the evening wandering around the streets and finally turning in back at the B&B.

In the morning I went back to the marina, slouched around the docks awhile, and stared at the old wooden sailboat now bobbing around under a gray and lifeless sky. I walked around her decks once more and examined the array of wood and metal whatnots hanging everywhere. Walking up the tar road to the marina building, I still hadn't formulated the right expression of regret in not offering to buy the boat. After some scrounging around, I found Long John Silver hiding out in his office. We sat there while I got up the nerve and finally said, "Ya know John? I'm thinking X dollars." It was a number that sort of popped out of my mouth after much bottled up consideration over the last night—it was semiautomatic, like a well rehearsed line in a play. That number, which will not be published here, was very well below the asking price. I reasoned that it addressed the obvious wear and tear, wouldn't exactly embarrass the lads in England, would buy Long John a dinner out, would float with Georgia—if I presented it right. It wouldn't drain the exchequer; it would send me home with money in my jeans. Long John got this little grin on his face.

Inwardly I did a double take, because I knew instantly that my number could have been lower—maybe even ridiculously lower! So my instinct had been correct. The lads only wanted to get rid of the boat. Maybe Long John just felt good about unloading what could be a long-term problem if nobody came to the rescue. Whatever, he produced the papers while I wrote a check for the down payment. Then I marched off for a last look before I flew back to Minneapolis. There she was, bobbing around in the gray water like a lost soul. I took some photos and then I headed up the road for the Baltimore airport.

Shipping a
Boat Overland

Back home Georgia and I dropped the film in a one-hour place and killed some time wandering around the local mall until the prints were ready. I couldn't wait for the images to see if my recollection of the boat's hidden charm was visible to someone beside myself. Actually, it was not. Even to me, those pictures really only magnified the bad condition she was in. It was impossible to see past the crap strewn around the interior. And the exterior shots—they seemed to dwell over much on blistered paint, raw, weather-worn brightwork, faded sail bags, and rat-gnawed rope. We both had to sit down while I searched for a logical line of defense. There was none. Nevertheless, true to form, Georgia gave the project the nod, though not as enthusiastically as I had anticipated.

A week later the lads accepted my offer. I rousted out the surveyor by phone and waited impatiently for his verdict. When he called to say she was structurally sound but had a couple of open seams—hence the leaking—I knew she was headed west, so money was exchanged and a cross-country boat transporter was contracted.

I had never shipped a boat overland before, so I was on pins and needles. Would she stay together over those many miles from the Chesapeake to St. Paul, or would she just rattle herself to flinders somewhere on the Pennsylvania Turnpike? Before they loaded her, of course, they un-stepped the mast, which was placed on a rack alongside the hull; since it stuck out past the boat, a red flag was attached to the end. There were lots of last-minute measurements to be sure the cabin top would clear the many bridges and elec-trical wires on the way. I held my breath every time the phone rang. I could just hear the voice on the other end of the phone if it did: "Well, Jack," I was afraid I might hear, "we've got a little problem." Finally the shipper called to say the truck—and the boat—would arrive in St. Paul the following morning.

On that damp, gray late September morning, we drove down the long hill from the bluff tops in St. Paul to the Mississippi River bottoms and the Watchamajig Marina to meet our boat. The big white truck carrying it had just ar-rived, and a small crowd of boatyard boys was gathering to see this exotic new arrival. On land she seemed much larger than I remembered. That's because of the huge amount of below-the-waterline lumber she came with; the sight of her sitting on the rails of our transport truck was breathtaking. I was especially pleased at the tight, fair planking on both sides of the hull. No big gaps, sprung planks, or hogged but-tocks. (Hogged buttocks, I have since learned, are sags in the bilges caused by weakened or broken frames. Hogged buttocks show up at several fast-food joints I frequent, but that's another story.)

The yard boys searched through the weedy pile of angle jacks near their overgrown fence line until they came up with a rusty and seldom-used steel cradle tall enough to reach the boat's bilge and long enough to support the forward section of the hull. Someone cranked up the old blue Travelift and steered it around into position behind the truck. It growled and spit exhaust smoke like an old dragon, but since it had plenty of exercise carrying boxy houseboats around the yard, I kept the faith. The boys attached the slings, and LILIBET came off the truck without incident. It was a thrill to see her hanging in the air and knowing she had sailed all by her lonesome from England to Bermuda to Annapolis, and now found at least a temporary home in St. Paul, Minnesota, where she would undergo a major refit. It was also a little scary.

Georgia and I walked around her as if she were a beached whale, rubbing her planks and taking pictures and trying to be cool in front of the yard guys while they puttered about with blocks and planks and wondered more than a little who this weird old guy in the Ralph Lauren sweatshirt was, anyway. Who would bring some exotic old museum piece into their little patch of proper boat junk and fiberglass river craft? What's the deal here? And how about the depth on that keel? How the heck is he going to run that thing in the river, not to mention any Minnesota lake except maybe Lake Superior—and hey, well, that's a pretty dicey place to sail. Especially for old people. This guy must be nuts!

Our daughter Jordan brought her dippy boyfriend along. He was a native St. Paul guy and surely thought the whole lot of us were crazy as bedbugs for spending good money on something so clearly impractical and labor intensive. That was okay. He'd be history soon (in the boyfriend department), and she already knew we were crazy, but she loved us anyway. I commented to one of the crew that I hoped to have the bottom redone by snow time. He laughed. "Well," he said, "you better hurry. That's only a couple of weeks away". That gave me pause, because I thought I remembered those long October autumns with plenty of time to get ready for winter. But then, perhaps I was thinking of Seattle. I shrugged it off and listened while thinking of the tasks ahead and making plans. That was on a Monday. It was hard to concentrate during the rest of the workweek.

Saturday, we arrived early at the boatyard to get started. We had stopped at the builder's supply store and picked up a stepladder so we could reach the deck for boarding. My list of work to be done began with unloading everything on board and inventorying what was worth keeping and what was junk. Of course everyone around me had to examine my throwaway pile as if it were treasure from the lost tomb, but I managed to dump quite a bit of trash anyway. We were amazed at the seemingly endless bundles of sodden and salty ropes and sails and books and cushions and life vests that kept turning up in every possible nook within the boat. There were tool boxes half full of water and crammed with rusty tools. There was rain gear hanging in the closet, zippers and buttons crusted stuck with green corrosion. Mixed in was all the standing and running rigging, politely wrapped and labeled by the yacht yard which had dismasted the boat prior to loading her onto the truck.

We lowered everything over the side with ropes and put it into the back of my pickup truck for transport to the studio over in Minneapolis, where it could be cleaned, dried, folded, refinished, and stored for the winter. We had four truckloads of stuff, including two spinnaker poles, an ensign pole, and a small staysail boom, all in need of major refinishing. The main boom remained on board where it had been lashed down for travel. The mast was put atop some 55-gallon drums nearby. I reminded myself to keep an eye on that thing to keep it safe from damage. I had brought a big worktable and my road box full of miscellaneous tools from the studio and set them next to the hull so I would have a work surface and a safe storage place for things needed at ground level. The good stuff—electric drills, saws, sanders, etc.—all went on board.

By Sunday afternoon my two-thousand-square-foot workspace on the third floor of an old brick warehouse close by where we live looked like a boatshop. Normally, I use this space to make paintings and sculptures and a variety of creative commercial jobs. For a good many years in my life, I designed and built what were termed industrial decorating projects for clients around the country. Hotels, shopping malls, and large-scale corporate events were most of my clients. Seasonal projects, especially Christmas decorations on a national scale, were also big on the job list. Large production space has always been a necessity, and since between or around commercial work, I make art, I call it my studio. I had recently retired from the decorating business, and this sea change was kind of nice.

Just now, things were pretty much of a jumble, but you could get a close look at the rigging, the sails, the poor old dodger—ratty and faded, with no visibility left in the plastic windows. I hung it from the rafters for future reference. There were books about plant life on Barbados, a chart for the ocean around Iceland and another for Long Island Sound, and a ports-of-call book for the Chesapeake Bay. There was a whole collection of pennants from many foreign ports, all beautifully weather-beaten. There were two sets of rubber foul-weather gear, one with the right leg cut off—probably the outboard side so as not to get fouled in the lifelines as the sailor moved along the deck. There were a wind generator on a long stick, boxes of water-hose clamps, a wad of cotton roving, a bag of oakum (or something like it), winch handles—all in very bad condition— duckboard racks (slats) from the sleeping berths, the original tiller, a manual bilge pump (that could be handy), and storm boards for the doghouse.

There, you see? I'm talking that silly sailor talk already; one might even get the impression I knew then what was going on, sailorwise. (The doghouse is actually a raised cabin just ahead of the cockpit into which you dive when headed down below. It has side and forward windows, which are covered with storm boards in heavy weather.)

Lines in a wide range of poor condition made up much of the plunder we retrieved from the boat that weekend. They had been coiled into large workmanlike bundles and were frozen in place by dried salt water; you could hold them straight out in front of you and they would still retain their shape. I hung them from the rafters. All together, this whole mess spread out in the studio emitted a lingering odor of diesel fuel and the sea.

Preparing for the Winter

Back in St. Paul, my first assignment was to strip the old paint from the bottom of LILIBET's hull below the waterline and apply a new coat of copper bottom paint before winter set in. I wanted to do this not so much because the boat really needed it. In retrospect, I think I could have just pressure-washed her and then used a good red bottom paint, but instead, I felt some need to get down to the true base of things. I suppose I needed to do some kind of hard labor to convince myself and those around me that this was no dilettante project, to demonstrate that I really meant business. So for the next month while the weather held, I spent every spare minute running a big old power disk sander up and down, back and forth, overhead, underhand from bow to stern and back again. You have to be very careful and focused to keep the disk from gouging into the wood. Thankfully, my early days of polishing big steel sculptures with exactly the same sort of machine gave me a leg-up on the process, but every now and then I left slight evidence of bad positioning, or fatigue, in the way of telltale swirls. Most of these I later eased out before painting. (Remember, this was below the waterline.)

*   *   *

The lads at the boatyard thought I was nuts, of course. Why not just hire Chip (the yard boss) to sandblast the son-of-a-gun? Actually, I didn't feel like being indebted to the yard guys just at the moment, and I felt a certain desire to be in control of my own project. Also, when I checked out the sandblasting machine and discovered it to be a giant old industrial monster about the size and shape of a Sherman tank, covered in rust and dirt, with air lines duct-taped together, I just couldn't bring myself to trust the ability of the yard boys to scrub that fine old hull without taking out most of the cotton caulking and lots of tight-fitting bungs, leaving me with more restoration work than I started with. So while our short fall slipped into early winter, my weekends were spent enveloped in red dust. I found I could complete about a quarter of the hull per weekend.

This, by the way, is a perfect time to discuss work schedules and methods. Examples of great intentions gone south are everywhere there are boats. I had long ago heard and read about the disaster of trying to accomplish too much boat restoration in too short a time. Just to underscore that idea, one of the first things the local expert said to us was, "Don't do too much at one time. Pick a spot and finish it." My own rule—even though I'm not an expert—has been to uncover only as much wood as I can cover before sundown, and I'm sticking to it.

The drill was to rough-sand down to bare wood and lay in seam compound where needed. Because the wood was still soaked with salt water from LILIBET's time at sea, not much old compound had dried and fallen out. In places

where it had I used a black marine underwater seam compound from a tube. After I had gotten about halfway
around the hull, Tearful Ted, one of the old boys at the
marina, convinced me to try something called 3M 5200.

It turns out that Ted was one of those people who are always lamenting things, always looking on the dark side. He
had a thirty-six-foot powerboat—a 1960s something-or-
other—and he was restoring it on the grass across the road
from my boat. He would wander over once or twice a day
to lament about paint not drying, screws not grabbing,
wood rotting, the sun beating down, worms that might eat
his boat. . . . Worms were a big worry for him, since he was
planning to move his boat via the Mississippi to Florida,
where he hoped to live out his days fishing from the after
deck. Wood-eating worms were a big problem in Florida.
After a while, I began to think of him as "Tearful Ted."

Watching me smooth in the black seam caulking compound, Tearful Ted began lamenting about how one just
couldn't trust these boat-store products that promise stuff
they don't deliver. His favorite expression—always delivered with a marvelously sad expression—was, "Yep, it's a
terrible thing to see them seams open up."

Well, sure, but Ted, guess what. Wood moves, seams
open. You recaulk them and soak the boat in the lake, the
ocean, whatever. The seams swell closed. This is good news,
not bad.

Still, he got me worried, and I bought some 5200. It's
white, although I've heard you maybe can get it in black if
you special-order it and have time to wait for delivery. It
also seemed to be more gluey than the caulking compound

I had been using, although it's probably just a slightly less dense kind of paste. I was a little suspect, because the cost of a tube of 5200 at the local builders' supply company was about half as much as the fancy black boat caulk I had started with, which probably says more about marketing and the American consumer than about the actual product. Since then, I've read that 5200 is pretty standard as a seam caulk, so I feel much better about using it. (Now I've gone back to the black boat stuff; it does seem to work better.)

After caulking, I wiped the hull down with acetone, waited till the caulk cured (overnight, most of the time), sanded again with a 4½-inch orbital disk sander, wiped her down with acetone once more and painted her. You have to be a little careful when sanding so as not to let the disk grab up

Refinishing the underside of LILIBET's rubrails, Spring 2003

any of that fresh caulk and pull it out. Because I remembered what we used on DENALI and thought I'd stay with tradition, I put on two coats of soft-surface copper bottom paint. Later, in the spring, I changed my mind and recoated the bottom with ablative hard-coat red copper. It looked a lot nicer.

Sanding bottom paint is probably the most awful job of any in boat work. The dust is more than slightly lethal, as it is full of copper and various other bad things, so I wore a dust mask and wrapped a towel around my throat to prevent dust from going down my shirt. I wore goggles some of the time, but because they steamed up and I couldn't see, I had to remove them. By noon I looked like a sweeper of red chimneys. I worked as fast as I dared, but it was still four weekends for the task. At the time of this project I was 59 years old and had spent much of the previous two years behind a desk at the art center where I direct programs. These two-day stints of hard toil were part of the grand scheme of physical rehabilitation by hard labor when I got started on the boat hunt. The physical activity felt great, and the shock to my unsuspecting system was almost humorous; that is, if you like pain. Nights were restful.

On one of those Saturdays early in the project, just before the bottom-painting phase, we decided to rig a cover for the topsides in preparation for winter. Good idea. Towards the end of October the weather gets ugly in Minnesota. It gets ready for winter in quick steps that go from wet, to cold and wet, to frozen.

We picked up a couple dozen one-inch-OD plastic PVC pipes. I think they were 12 feet long. We also bought two bags of electrical zip ties and two giant blue plastic painter's tarps. Starting at the bow and working aft, one of us on each side, we cut the pipes to appropriate lengths and bent them in hoops to form a tent frame above the decks and cabin. The hoop ends were tied using the zip ties to the lifeline stanchions along the toerails. At the apex of our hoop framework, we ran a straight pipe the length of the boat and built supports at intervals using blocks of wood from around the yard. Over this structure we stretched the blue tarps, and I roped them tight from side to side under the keel. Meanwhile, Georgia had stitched up some beautiful canvas bags to hold sand. These were to be hung from the bottom edge of the tarps, with the sand providing weight to keep the tarps tight. Somehow we got sidetracked, and the bags didn't get used. As it turned out, however, the tarps and ropes did well over the winter.

"So, yer hoopin' it," the local wooden boat expert said after giving it the fish eye when he saw us building the structure. His tone was "been there, done that" gloomy, and it made me think maybe I really better forget the whole boat project. But the hoops held up gallantly, with only occasional puddles of melted snow forming and freezing, causing the plastic cover to dish; I dumped them overboard on my weekend visits throughout the winter.

Just about the time when we were building our little hoop tent, along came some old friends, a married couple, to see the boat. Like me, Steve is a not so young sculptor and he is trying out architecture school in what many folks hereabouts might call a classic left turn.

Think of it. Years of work in the studio—and good work at that, bending and welding metal—suddenly moved to the back burner in order to study engineering charts, load limits versus cantilevered decking versus earth stress factors, good design versus good client relations, and, worst of all, math. All this while handing out the usual 21st-century handsome tuition fees to do it. Wow! Like paying for moorage. I like it already, but I bet he got plenty of funny looks down at Gopher's Tap when he made the announcement. "Go back-to-school to do what?" It all fits snugly into the philosophy of change, doesn't it? Maybe that's why we have had this long-term friendship.

My friend's wife is a successful fabric colorist. She runs a fabric-dyeing shop out of her studio in their house. They sometimes take vacations on sailboats. They are also bicyclists, so they cycled over to the boatyard wearing all the current regalia of the cycling world. It was interesting to see this colorful array of spandex and wire wheels come cycling through the rows of old and tired wooden hulls.

I sometimes wonder what people expect to see on a boatyard inspection of this sort—probably things of a "yacht-like" nature, such as ropes and anchors and lots of gleaming white shippy-looking bows topped with honey-colored mahogany and rows of polished-brass portholes. I was wishing for some of that as I watched them pedal nearer, because I knew that's what my little boat would look like one day, but at the moment, only I could imagine it. On some obscure level where there's boats, there's sure to be a boaty atmosphere, but on a slightly overcast fall day on the river bottoms down here in what can only be called a working boatyard, most of the nifty stuff is covered with blue plastic, disassembled for repair, or just isn't there at all. Plus, there's really no way to prepare the uninitiated landlubber for the terrors of a restoration project like this one. It's a little like looking into the interior of a wrecked auto in a junkyard. The sheer scale of the project can be overwhelming.

Climbing aboard was a struggle. The boat was ultra dirty from her past months in Maryland and the big road trip, plus the boatyard was like a dirt pit in a wind storm, so things were pretty dicey for these two members of the Minneapolitan urban gentry who had only minutes ago been pedaling placidly along the metropolitan parkways, surrounded by old elms and oak trees and like-minded bikers, runners, joggers, and dog walkers. I hadn't yet brought in an extension ladder, so everyone had to boost themselves onto a big wooden work bench and then up a six-foot stepladder balanced on top of the bench to reach the decks.

They climbed aboard and wrinkled their noses at the diesel smell, wrestled the blue plastic tarps aside, and stepped down gamely into the saloon. It was cold and dark, and it was pretty clear that they recognized a big, fat, risky project when they saw one. "Wow, this is a lot of work!"

I did the nickel tour of the interior, trying not to linger on anything long enough to generate too much public scrutiny, talked about the boat's history, and suggested that I would remove most of the existing interior to make room for some creature comforts. They agreed to that plan.

The local wooden boat expert, who by now we can call Clark, arrived and joined us for a look-see. He was cautiously optimistic. We chatted things up for awhile until the chill of damp wood and dim light drove us over the side and down to ground level, where my friends' bikes gleamed in the early twilight. All in all, it was a little awkward because the overwhelming but unspoken question (as usual with these kinds of undertakings) was, "Are you sure you can do this, Jack?" The answer, of course, must always be "Most certainly I'm sure," even though you're not. Projects like this require lots of self-confidence.

As everyone knows, boats and boat projects like this one have a way of stirring up the imagination. So it wasn't much of a surprise when several weeks later my friend Steve and I crossed paths, and he offered to help me redesign and build the interior of my boat. I was cautious. I'm an under-the-radar type of operator when it comes to big-bite projects. I had already promised Georgia that I had enough fortitude and focus to complete this thing before it became an embarrassment.

For me, however, focus is a solitary endeavor and requires certain acts of accomplishment that other people might consider outrageous. Such as using tools for other purposes than they were meant for. Or worse yet, delaying the purchase of the correct tool while trying to get the job done with a monkey wrench.

And I was relishing the concept of having a nice, long, private restoration affair with this sweet little yacht. I was looking forward to those long hours of solitude inside the hull while I pondered the right and the wrong way to remove some contrary old bronze screw from a particularly difficult location. I had in mind to test my own design skills in this first-time stab at rebuilding a boat interior, and I wanted to prove to myself that I could indeed accomplish the task.

Still, Steve's offer was genuine and well meant, so I smiled and gave him a positive nod. Privately, I predicted that this could be rather like a St. Paul remake of *Grumpy Old Men*, because while golfing likes to be a group activity, as do bowling and poker and croquet and picnics, restoring an old boat is often a lonesome activity. It doesn't have to be—there are schools and groups and historic preservation committees, etc., and yes, the occasional buddy project—but I've done enough of it now to say with some certainty that for me the joy of diddling about on my boat project while I learn and discover and progress at my own pace, using the simple tools at hand for long periods of peaceful uninterrupted work time, is just an unsurpassed joy. I was reluctant to give it up. I know Steve understood, because after some initial good faith attempts to make joint progress, he sort of disappeared from the screen. It was a considerate thing to do and I appreciate it to this day.

By now the weather was getting pretty bad in a consistent way, and I rushed along on the bottom, grinding and painting, holding my breath for a few 50-degree afternoons before the snow came. The giant keel had also become quite a curiosity to the boatyard crowd. Word of her history had got about, and folks were naturally curious, although few stopped to chat. I think they could sense the urgency in my methods. Sometimes cars would slow down as they drove past, and the passengers would all crane their necks to see the mad sanding man wrapped in dusty red rags flailing away with his heavy disk grinder under the curves of the hull. Every so often someone would ask about the trip across the Atlantic, and I would have to tell them it wasn't me. That always made the chatter die. I worked on.

When I finally completed the job just in the nick of time, I began a long series of winter weekends under the tarps working on the interior. The temperature dropped into the 40s, then 30s (that's degrees Fahrenheit). I scheduled an engine winterization with the boatyard. Here in the north, all the boats come out of the water in October, and for the next couple of weeks they get an antifreeze run through so they don't freeze up. If they have sealed cooling systems, antifreeze gets dumped in, as in a car. If they are raw-water cooled like mine, meaning water from the lake or the ocean in which you are floating is pumped through the engine block and discharged back into the pond, cooling the engine as it passes, they just run some antifreeze through the engine and drain it out.

The diesel engine that was installed in LILIBET had been running a couple of weeks earlier when Long John had motored the six or so miles from his marina to the yacht yard that pulled LILIBET out of Chesapeake Bay for the truck ride to St. Paul, so I knew the boys at Watchamajig could get her running again. They did. On my next work weekend, I pumped and drained all the freshwater pipes I could find and pumped the big old belly tank as dry as I could get it with an electric transfer pump I found at the builders' supply depot. Then I kept my fingers crossed as the temperature dropped more.

With the addition of the plastic winter covering, boarding and entering the boat had now become a torturous exorcise: climbing up the ladder, over the lifelines, under the tarps, along the decks, over the cockpit coaming, into the cockpit, and finally down into the dark, cold, and diesel-saturated interior. That crawl down the decks was always dirty and bruising—hey, and we weren't even at sea yet.

I stretched a power cord from the barn to the boat, so I could plug in lights, a heater, and tools. As winter progressed, the heater could just about take off the big chill, although on sunny days the plastic acted like a greenhouse and helped take the deep freeze away. Sometimes you might not quite see your breath, but it was always cold in there and the work progressed at a snail's pace—not just because of the cold, but also because it took me a long time to form a plan of attack. My greatest fear was to find myself with a big, costly project out of control, so I became extremely deliberate and thankful that these first efforts were well hidden from public exposure and dockyard judgment. Occasionally the power would go off and the whole exit-entry thing would have to be undertaken so I could reset the breaker back on the barn wall. Jordan gave me a boom-box for Christmas, and I could play some tunes while I worked. Georgia announced that she was a fair weather boat worker so I was on my own for the season. The days had grown short, and things slowed even more.

Winter Work

Essentially, the work involved removing everything from the main saloon so I could get the inside of the hull cleaned and painted prior to rebuilding. An interesting note along the way was that when I first began the project, I remember thinking how austere and cramped the space inside the hull seemed to be. Every step along the dark saloon, every turn of the body resulted in some form of bruise on the shins, the head, elbows, and lots of other protruding places. As time and work progressed, though, I began to get adjusted to the small space. Indeed it did help to remove some of the old panels that constricted movement, but in time I began to feel at ease within the space and this ease has actually turned to a certain form of comfort in the finished project of today. I guess the adaptability of human nature fits in somewhere here.

Since the entire interior was going to be reconfigured, I felt no obligation to save much of the Spartan furnishings, and thus there was a lot of heave-ho from under the tarps. Besides that, even with the greatest care, the most undivided attention and the most deliberate handling of tools, the removal of sixty-five-year-old screws and cabinet backing was sometimes less than perfect. And then when these carefully preserved parts were finally removed and examined for future use, it was mostly clear that they would certainly have no part in the greater scheme of things. Unless I was willing to simply rebuild the interior as it was originally built, no amount of reshaping, gluing, drilling, or screwing would make their presence any better than new, well-made cabinetry—and Zen screw removal in the belly of this boat was not happening. This means that occasionally the sound of wrenching timbers could be faintly heard across the frozen boatyard, along with a good string of the King's English. Still I was always successful at keeping the structural members of the hull totally unharmed.

My goal was to only do one section of the interior at a time, and given the short working hours allowed, my immediate focus was the saloon only. That included removal of the engine box, the companionway steps (the stairway leading down below from the cockpit), the galley sink and stove—along with the cabinetry around them—the hot-water heater, freshwater pump (a green lump covered with corrosion), the settee frames and supports, the cabin sole, and most important, the two diesel tanks made of rusted steel, and leaking.

That explained the bad odor. Each tank held approximately 50 gallons of fuel, and while each had only a few gallons of diesel left, they had to be pumped empty before I could get them off the boat. A job. The empty tanks were then levered up over the engine, out into the cockpit, and finally up and over the side, where they dove to earth with a

big thud. By the end of it I looked like a street person without a shopping cart; the folks in my apartment building elevator turned the other way when I showed up. Probably
thought I would ask for money.

With the tanks out, the space became easier to deal
with. Some serious cleaning and attempted painting began.
As for the paint part, I stuck to basic covering of a cleaned
hull with navy gray and used a revolutionary old product
called Rustoleum. It dries rock hard even in chilly temperatures, somewhat slowly, doesn't peel, and covers all kinds
of bad crud. Progress was being made. By January 1, I had
a sense of accomplishment, even if I was the only one who
could see it. I also began to wake up in the night worrying
about the putting-back-together part.

One night late I found some medium-weight smooth
cardboard gift boxes left over from Christmas. Georgia
likes to save packaging—Lord knows when there could be
a run on cardboard just when you might need a gift box. I
lifted it quietly to my tiny library and started in with a pair
of scissors and a glue gun, creating a model of the saloon
section of my boat. For the next week, I clipped and glued,
feeling my way along the path to a new interior layout.

Keeping things in relative scale was difficult. It would
be so easy to make little cabinets and tables and seating
modules that worked perfectly in the tight little cardboard
cabin—if only people measured no more than three feet
tall. Little by little however, by week's end I had devised a
close approximation of the cabin design I finally built. For
the time being, this exercise gave me great piece of mind

and a feeling of control over the project. I knew I could build it. With the cardboard model complete, I put it on a low bookshelf and went back to work on the real thing with renewed vigor.

January always drags along. The snow banks turn gray, the sky stays heavy most of the time, and much of Minnesota goes south to Florida. For the rest of us the convention center in Minneapolis has its big boat show. It comes at a time when everyone is yearning for sun and fun on the water, of course. I had never before attended. My architect/artist friend called to enquire if we should go together, so Georgia and I gladly accepted. Predictably, the Minnesota boat show was a monument to aluminum fishing boats, Skidoos, runabouts, and pontoon party barges. It's what we do here (most of us), and the crowd was full of fishermen looking for that ideal electronic fishfinder advertised at the "boat show special" price. Marinas up and down the Mississippi were selling slip space, and I checked all of them out. Everyone was a little nonplussed when I described my boat; a few were sympathetic, while a few others were just a smidge sarcastic. Looking at the shallow draft on all those lake boats perched on their little angle jacks did give me a fresh case of nerves about water depth for sailboats.

We climbed aboard the sailboats and toured all the molded, rounded, stacked, bolstered, fitted, modular, padded, prefabricated, and polished interior spaces. They are wonderful and certainly reflect the modern sailor's desire for comfort. Double sinks, stove tops, refrigerators with freezers, ovens, molded shower stalls, cozy little heads with nifty built-in places for all those homey knicks and knacks. Ruffled curtains, double-squishy cushions on everything, giant beds, recessed lighting—wow! It's like a powerboat. I'm home! Quite a difference from the stern and soggy little saloon over there on LILIBET. After an hour or so, we all got bored with the show and found our way back out into the leaden Minnesota winter.

January weather finally won out, and I had to trim my weekend work at the boatyard to quick visits just to check on the covering and monitor the drying-out progress of the hull planks. The boat was supersaturated with seawater when we brought her in, and she dried out very slowly. Sometimes I would find a thin layer of ice on some of the lower sections where water was still seeping out of the wood when the sun hit the hull. Here and there some seams were beginning to open a little. I redirected my work to the studio back in Minneapolis, where I separated all the piles of boat stuff into categories and built a 4- by 8-foot worktable. I ran out and got a new miter saw, an orbital disk sander, a drill, a saber saw, sandpaper, and some new hand tools. Also a bunch of throw away brushes and some paint and varnish (Helmsman high gloss). I was ready to go.

The biggest spinnaker pole caught my eye first. It's about 12 feet long and 4 or 5 inches in diameter, with a big old bronze spring-loaded hook on one end. It was covered with a peeling gray varnish skin, and had a lot of exposed wood and some open lesions along the run of the grain. I sanded it clean, filled the cracks, and varnished it. Each night for the rest of the week I stopped at the studio on my way home from work and lightly sanded the pole and gave it another coat of varnish. By the end of the week the surface felt like glass and looked great.

Most weekends in January and February were spent in the shop refinishing pieces of the old boat. I also built a new set of companionway steps, and floor coverings for the engine box and its adjacent flooring sections. The inside of the hull had been ceiled with mahogany—that is, lined with strips of wood laid horizontally along the face of the frames. There were gaps between the strips, which allowed air to circulate but gave the inside of the boat a rather cell-like feeling and provided lots of dirt-catching nooks and a lot of up close and personal contact with the hull.

I removed all these ceiling strips, took them over to the studio, and reused them for the cockpit sole (that's the floor of the cockpit) by gluing and screwing them to the old sole beams and giving them a darn good caulking with plenty of spar varnish over. It was easy to do, they looked super in their new role, and the result gave me lots of confidence in my woodworking skills.

The cabin doors were refinished, and the splash boards that fit just below the cabin doors went from faded yellow peeling varnish to nice, deep mahogany with brass handles. The ensign pole got the treatment, as did the original tiller. The latter, by the way, has a carved dogs' head—a faithful old hound—on the inboard end. It was probably carved by the shipwright who built the boat; it could have been a reminder that, along with the dog, the hand-steered tiller is man's best friend, or it could have been nothing more than the image of a salty old dog as decoration.

Meanwhile, we looked at our sail inventory. The main and the small staysail—the basic working sails—were faded maroon in color. Both were in pretty fair condition, so there was to be no trading out just yet; besides, we liked the color—especially when we thought about how new, unfaded sails in the same color would look. Especially with that soon-to-be-black hull. Too bad the rest of the sail inventory was white. Either way both colors would work with a black sailboat—perhaps not at the same time, but we figured we would cross that bridge when we got there. We picked a nice, deep, burgundy-brown color from a sample chart, and Georgia got enough fabric to make new sail bags and sail covers. She stitched up the bags in her homework room, and they are wonderfully pro.

The next four weekends were spent cleaning the sails. Leave it to the beavers to get themselves into mega projects that would be a lot easier if they just waited for good weather. Minnesota, however, has lots of bad, cold weather, and if you wait too long, nothing much gets done. This was February, and the outside temperature was around 10 to 20 degrees. We cleared the studio floor, laid down a lot of construction-grade poly sheeting and then picked a sail from the big folded mess in the corner and stretched it out on the poly. We hauled buckets of water on the freight elevator from the public rest rooms. Starting at the foot of the sail—that is, the bottom edge—and using our new supply of super soap, which we had purchased at the boat show, we washed our way to the head—that is, the top. Saturdays we spent all day scrubbing sails. All the sails were big, but a couple were huge. We have a genoa sail that covered the entire floor space and, when wet, weighed a lot. The drill was to suds and scrub down one, side rinsing as we went, but leaving plenty of water and soap in the fabric, then turning the sail over and repeating the process. It took most of the day because the fabric was full of salt and grime, and there were splotches of mold stains here and there. In the end we rolled and folded the wet sail into a soaking bundle wrapped in plastic and hauled it on a dolly down the freight elevator to the loading dock, where we heaved it into the bed of our pickup truck. We did this one sail at a time, because each sail was a Saturday project by itself.

Leaving the studio, we drove the wet sail six blocks to our apartment building. By the time we arrived in our garage, the sail would be frozen, so we let it sit in the bed of the truck overnight. Because the garage is heated, the package would be workable in the morning. On Sunday morning, then, we would drive the truck into our garage car wash and unfold the sail in the bed of the truck, all the while spraying the daylights out of it to rinse out the dirt and soap. What a job. Suds flowed from the sail and covered the garage floor. It went pretty well, though—the garage hose had a pressure head, and while the sails didn't come out snow white, they did lose their gray color and all of the built-up salt that clung to the fabric. We also got a clean truck out of the deal. After the rinse, we walked around on the refolded bundle to squeeze as much water out as we could and then brought it to the studio, where we hung the wet, slightly frosty sail from the rafters to dry.

We always went to bed stiff and sore after those sessions. How simple it would have been to lay the sails out on the grass somewhere and spray them down with a hose while sudsing and brushing. But remember, folks, Minnesota winters are long and we are urban dwellers with no convenient lawn or garden hose. There's a saying in this state: "Whatever works."

March brought just an ever-so-slight lessening of the deep freeze, and I took up the tarp crawl again to begin building a framework to support the first part of my new interior reconfiguration, using my cardboard model as a guide. I was very relieved to be working on this part by myself, because these first steps needed a lot of mulling over. That means I spent much time just standing around in the empty hull eyeballing the shape of things. Finally, I bought some one-inch Styrofoam sheets and began to cut out pattern pieces, which I taped together with duct tape into a variety of modular possibilities. It was slow going but by the end of the second weekend, I had a beginning. This was typical of my working style, and certainly frustrating to those who know me. I work from a conceptual overview, not a detailed step-by-step approach. I have trouble with too many details up front clogging the passages of creative thinking. This approach could be bad news in the boatbuilding world and a good reason why I may never actually build a boat from scratch. LILIBET was a boat that gave me a structure within which I could be creative in a controlled way.

*   *   *

By early April, I had the first seating modules installed, and a solid floor unit under the companionway ladder. To make this happen, I had stripped out every scrap of the old cabinetry that had been the stove compartment and the icebox and the sink counter. This sounds like a lot, but the scraps made a decidedly small pile on the ground when I heaved them overboard.

Choosing my path for rebuilding carefully, I first cleaned and painted the bilge underneath the section of floor—the sole, in sailor talk—where the new companionway steps from the cockpit would be. I had built the new steps over in my studio, and had shaped and finished the new oak floor planking that they would land on; they were just waiting for this framework. Building a framework to carry this flooring and attach it to the old structural members of the boat was the first challenge. I had to make sure the new installation didn't interfere with the old, such as hoses and wires and through-hull fittings, which had to have enough clearance so they didn't get built in and become trapped, inoperable and unrepairable, The new framing had to be solid and tight, or the flooring resting on it would bump and grind every time someone stepped on it. And the new flooring had to fit easily onto the frame so it could be removed for inspection, cleaning, and repairs to the machinery down there in the bilge. When there's smoke or an odd noise or water or steam coming up from the bilge through seams in the floor planking, you have to be able to jerk that section of flooring up and away so you can get to the trouble. Or at the very least you need to remove that flooring to clean the bilge every so often.

The floor frame gave me a first look at the beginnings of the redesign of the entire saloon. Funny how your eye will imagine how everything follows once you put down the first few boards. I framed up the new seating modules on either side of the new floor framework.

Outside, the boatyard was showing signs of spring. Sporadic snow melt turned the ground soft; little rivulets of water ran from everywhere down toward the river. On certain days I could leave the cabin doors open to the plastic-covered cockpit and pick up some astonishing warmth from the greenhouse effect as the sun pelted down on the blue plastic.

Finally it was time to cover the seating frames. I went with three-quarter-inch plywood finished on both sides with three coats of gloss white enamel and screwed tightly to the frames. The sitting part of the seats had to be removable, so I put an inch-and-a-half hole in each near the front so you could place a finger or two into the hole and lift off the seat top. Clean, white surfaces looked pretty good after so many weeks of clutter. I thought for a minute I could get away with painted plywood surfaces, but all that loose grain was unnerving so I decided to cover it with a screwed and glued birch veneer. The birch is really smooth and gives a tight, unified look to the finished job. Additionally, I trimmed the seating, and every other bit of cabinetry in the interior of the boat, with oak outside corner molding.

At this point I realized that I needed to get those fuel tanks replaced before I could proceed with the rest of the interior. In the original layout, the tanks were laid along the length of the saloon on both sides of the hull. They were held in place by the framing for settees, which faced each other across the center aisle. That resulted in a rigid and uncomfortable little sitting room that collected loose stuff without pity. I was determined to change that. With the discovery of leakage along the bottom edge of the starboard tank and a thick crust of flaking rust on both tanks, I knew their replacement was a must. Now was the time to change either their shape or size, or move them.

Because tanks took up much of the floor space in the saloon, everything else, such as the galley sink—a pitiful little splash pan—and the propane stove, had been crammed aft on either side of the companionway ladder. This made for a jumble of confusion and affected how one functioned in the aft part of the saloon. For instance, the sink was adjacent to the engine gauges, which were only readable by climbing down the ladder into the saloon, then turning around to face the stern and bending way down next to the sink cabinet with hands on knees to peer at the little gauges.

Meanwhile, of course, the helm might be left unattended (if you were alone) just so you could check the oil pressure or engine temperature gauge. (What I didn't know until later was that none of the gauges really worked, so to the former owners, I guess, none of this mattered.) The engine starter switch, the battery gauges, and more were similarly obscured. Half of these important instruments were on the starboard side of the ladder and half were on the port side right next to the bottom of the propane stove. I suppose it might be helpful to keep an eye on the oil pressure while cooking stew, but it seemed to me a revision was in order.

After much consideration and sketching during quiet moments here and there, I decided to locate the new tanks right where the old ones were but to shorten them by a foot. This doesn't sound like much, but it opened great possibilities in a very small space. Shortening the tanks would cut their capacity by, oh, say ten gallons each, but that would still give me about eighty gallons of diesel on board. We would still be in good shape.

Now right here I must mention that quite a lot of my can-do attitude about this project relied on the industrial resources of the greater Twin Cities, where I lived. I was thinking that here in the heartland of America, where farms melded with manufacturing, one would simply peruse the yellow pages and out would pop a medley of welders ready to fry some metal.

Not so. Simple things, such as welding up a couple of new stainless-steel fuel tanks, easily arranged perhaps in Seattle, or Boston, or a hundred other seacoast towns—well frankly, I had the hardest time finding anyone to do the job. I kept running into a high degree of specialization, none of which included stainless-steel fuel tanks for a sailboat. Nowadays, I was informed, you buy preformed plastic tanks and strap them to the framing with a couple of nylon seat belts. Or so it seemed.

Lucky for me, the shop boys at Watchamajig heard the grumbling and said they could do it. I was impatient to get the cabin rebuilt and the tanks were holding things up, so I made a deal with the boatyard guys who seemed anxious to make some money. It was the first of several passes at using the locals and turned out to be something of a tribulation, but for now I was off and running.

The new shorter tanks were to be built exactly like the old ones, and they were to be pressure tested. All this was to take about two weeks' time. That was around the first of March. On June 23 the tanks were finally finished. Only three and three-quarters months later, and just one round of bad words between me and the yard boss. Not bad. Well, the good news was that by the time I started getting alarmed by the delay, the weather broke for spring and I could go back to the outside hull work. The interior could wait.

The new bottom paint had sluffed off pretty badly over the winter with all the water running off the plastic canvas and down the sides. Also to my horror, the seams of the planking were opening up all along the length of the boat. I knew this was a natural phenomenon for a wooden boat, but still it made my skin crawl. It was made worse by Tearful Ted, who would scuffle by on his way somewhere and tell me what an awful thing it was to see the seams open on a boat—and on and on about his old sailing days. Great. The first good weather weekend found me doing a speed grind on the bottom below the waterline to remove all the loose scale and then recaulking the open seams.

*   *   *

I had been haunted all winter long by a conversation with the expert about waterlines. He had eyed my fall work and commented about how little freeboard—the region from the waterline to the deck edge—there was. "Is that where the waterline really is?" he asked. Well shoot! I had researched my photos of the boat in the water, and I had ground off the bottom paint up to where a band of sludge ended at the white topsides. I had found what looked like a faint scribe line just at that height and followed it around the hull as I sanded. It was a true and good line—at least it sure seemed right by me—but this observation got me nervous. I got even more nervous when I discovered another faint scribe line about eight inches below the original. This one was now covered with copper bottom paint, but as I followed it along the length of the hull, there was no doubt as to its trueness.

So now I had two scribe lines. Which one was the right one?

I dithered on this before I made a decision. Either way, if I guessed wrong, there would be plenty of laughs from the peanut gallery. Finally, after a microscopic examination of those well-worn photos taken in Maryland, I stayed with the original line and kept going. By Sunday afternoon I was finished with the speed grind and gave the bottom a coat of ablative red copper. It looked great.

The following weekend Georgia rejoined the force and attacked the cockpit with a vengeance. She sanded down the big handrails along the coaming and also did the brightwork along the top of the coaming. She followed up by stripping down the old white interior of the cockpit, and patching and repainting. Then she refinished the big oak cockpit seats.

By now people in the marina recognized that we were serious about our project and began to say hello when they saw us. Some even overcame their skepticism about that big old sailboat over there and stopped to chat for a minute or two. Everyone asked where we were going to sail it. I was vague in my answers.

Spring Activity

The end of April and some days in May were typically wet that year, 2003, and most weekends were interrupted by rain. Still, we made it a routine to leave the house around 9 a.m. on Saturday and Sunday and work till 6 or 7 p.m.—especially as the days got longer and things began to green up. By mid-May we were on a roll. Starting at the tip of the slipper heel on the very after end of the boat and working from the top step of my trusty old aluminum stepladder, I ground off all the white topsides paint down to bare wood, working my way forward. I used mostly an orbital disk sander and a putty knife to strip off the scales of old paint. I would get a pretty big section stripped, and then I would patch the seams and fill in dings. I used mostly epoxy filler for the rough digs and dings, such as where old filler had fallen out of screw holes or some hard object had adjusted the fairness of the hull. Then before moving ahead, I would paint the bare wood with about three coats of gray primer. Sometimes the new paint would show an uneven sanding work, and I'd have to go back and smooth things out, and repaint.

As the weather got better and better, I began to take a

Friday off from my professional work every so often and go to the boatyard. This would give me three days straight to make some progress. By June 1, I had the entire hull primed, and by then my intentions to paint the hull black from deck edge to boottop were getting around the marina.

It got started when the expert asked me what color I would paint her, and I mentioned black. He then launched into the Herreshoff law of hull color.

Herreshoff was one of this country's premier yacht designers—a sainted master whose famous yard in Bristol, Rhode Island, turned out a large number of very successful sailing yachts. Most wooden boatmen take his words as gospel. Lucky for me I had read the guy's famous quote regarding paint color. It goes like this: "There are only two colors to paint a boat. One is white and the other is black, and only a fool would paint his boat black."

As the expert quoted Herreshoff's law, I joined in and we recited the punch line together, much to his surprise. I then added that nothing had stopped me from being foolish in the past, so why should I let it stop me now? We both got a good laugh. Not long afterward, word spread around the barns that that goofy sailor guy was going to paint his boat black.

The last thing I had to do, though, before I could paint the hull black was to make one last pass at a definitive location for that damned boottop. I took one last look through all the pictures I could find to see about how much space there was between the waterline and the deck edge, and in the end it was still a crap shoot. I determined to stay with the higher scribe line but to add another boottop under the one originally planned so I would have a double. Off I went with renewed faith in my heart.

Taping prior to painting is a fun job, and it's easy. When you add that blue masking tape to the project, you just know there's going to be some major progress, and sure enough when you pull it off, there is your new bootstripe— clear and clean. All of a sudden the boat takes on a leaner, more graceful look.

With a black hull in my mind, I had decided to do the boot in ivory. It seemed like a classic touch. Since I pretty much knew the scribe line was dead-on true, I simply followed it with the blue tape and measured from there up for my next tape line. The boottop actually was made up of three stripes: an inch-and-a-quarter ivory stripe below, a three-quarter-inch black stripe next up, and a two-inch ivory stripe on top. Above that, everything would be black to the deck rails, which of course would be varnished oak.

Finishing the boottop work was really exciting, because it left me nowhere to go but to the black hull paint. I started at the bow and worked aft along the port side to the transom, wiping the primed planking as I went with a weak solvent to get rid of all the dust and spreading on the black gold. In true belief that all my prep work had left the hull fair as a baby's bottom, I pressed on, impatient for that first glimpse from a distance.

What a shock I had. Even though I already knew this

fact, I was rudely reminded that the safest bet about black paint is the amount of detail it reflects. Standing back to admire my work made me cringe in disbelief at how much out of whack the surface of my boat seemed to be. There were bumps and dips and little chinks where every slight ding in the surface showed. This would not do!

The first term that sprang to mind was "fairing compound." I did some quick research in the boat supply catalogs without much luck, thinking I would find some magic salve that cures all ills. Then I pored over the chapters on finish techniques in my growing library of boat repair and building books. Nothing really definitive jumped out, so in the middle of the night I decided the exact right fairing compound must be Bondo, a type of polyester putty reinforced with glass fibers. After all, I had once made an entire car body out of the stuff. So the next day I got a gallon of Bondo and rough sanded the finished black paint down enough to apply it. Using a plastic paint spreader, I skinned the pink body putty over the surface of the hull. Now, we're not talking gobs and inches like cake frosting. This was just a very thin skin of body putty slicked across the dings, leaving enough in the various depressions to smooth them out. It was a dusty mess to sand it down again, but the results were amazing. Now it was time again to repaint the black. I don't know why exactly, but here I decided in my little artist's brain that I would try an experiment.

The best boat paint I could find is a product called Toplac by Interlux. It's advertised in all the yacht magazines as the latest in high-gloss, hard-finish, long-lasting, no-fade color for your topsides. I bought four quarts at $32 each. Then, just because I love the wonderful risk of the unknown, I bought four quarts of gloss black Rustoleum at $8 each. You guessed it. I painted one side with Toplac and one side with Rustoleum. They both looked exactly the same. After all the prep work I had just done, I felt a little guilty trying some dumb trick like this, but I couldn't help it. When you spend this much time so close to the boards, they begin to lose their precious heavenly "don't breath on 'em wrong" aura, and it just feels good to play around a little. Now we would wait and see what the season brings.

Once those coats of black paint went on, things got pretty friendly at the boatyard. I knew that hull would look great in black, and with the double boottop painted ivory, we got lots of compliments. Herreshoff's law of hull color never came up again.

By the end of June we were hard at it on the topside brightwork, and everyone was asking about a launch date. I burned out my orbital disk sander just as I reached the last two feet of high wooden bulwarks at the bow. Georgia completely restored the cockpit and cockpit coaming. A few weeks earlier she had discovered the power of wood hardener in a plastic syringe. She injected LILIBET's coaming and cabin tops like a veterinarian working on a giant sick animal. As the rhythm of the work took hold, we spent little time talking and lots of time bent in dusty single-minded absorption, coming to rest momentarily in the mid afternoon to slug down a cold soda. We hadn't been so sun-tanned since moving up from Florida six years previously. Evenings would find us early to bed.

Soon it was apparent that the boat must get into the water. The movement of planks under an old scruffy coat of paint matters naught, but when she starts to move right after a good paint job, and you know it's because of the sun and air—but the water is just across the street—well, you'd better go for it. The question of water depth now moved from the back burner to the front of the stove. The yard guys seemed anxious to get going on the launch, but when you really listened to them, it became apparent that they were a little unsure as to the process.

There is a long concrete ramp leading down to the water at the launch site. This was built to facilitate self-launching of the many trailer-hauled weekend boats used on the river. It also is used by the marina Travelift to launch the big houseboats and the occasional 40- to 50-foot power yacht. The old blue Travelift picks these boys up with straps under the hull and drives down the ramp into the water until the boat floats. Usually the low-draft cruisers float right away, and the lift hardly gets its feet wet. LILIBET has this big draft. It's seven feet to the boottop; she doesn't start to float until she's in six feet of water. The Travelift has an engine that bottoms out at five feet of water. Problem. If you drive the Travelift deeper than five feet, you begin to submerge the engine. The river was high just now because of heavy rain, so the thought was that it would be easier to get her in now without hitting bottom. The whole thing looked iffy to me, but these guys seemed confident.

Other boat freaks gathered round from their separate restoration projects scattered around the marina. Everyone talked about it. One guy said I didn't have a prayer—and he was a marina employee. Tearful Ted said not to trust anyone but Chip with the Travelift. Excitement built as I postponed the launch for a week while I pillaged supply stores for hose fittings, turnoff valves, rubber pipes, and connectors to stop up everything that might leak.

Our apartment was a tense place to be. We looked out the window and watched the river. Was it going lower? The 12-volt batteries that I had stored in the studio now sat on the apartment balcony plugged in to the charger and simmered away. One was a double-sized monster that must have weighed two hundred pounds. On launch day I would have to hoist them all onto the boat and hook them up to the bilge pump.

On the hot afternoon of launch, while I heaved and grunted the batteries up the sagging extension ladder to the deck, a passing yard guy said, "Hey, ain't you a little long in the tooth for that kind of thing?"

I wondered darkly what that old British sailor Francis Chichester of GIPSY MOTH IV fame would have said in reply. He had circumnavigated the world singlehanded on GIPSY MOTH IV when he was in his late sixties, and he was still ocean sailing by himself when he was in his seventies. I doubted any of these folks had ever heard of Chichester, so I just kept pushing and finally heaved the batteries one after the other onto the deck, and then slowly bullied them below into their parking spaces next to the diesel engine. I wired them up with my best electrical-engineering guess, and when I turned the old key, at least the amp gauge showed some life.

Just in case the batteries couldn't handle the load of LILIBET's pump when she went into the water, I had purchased a 110-volt sump pump that was rated for an outrageous amount of output and a 100-foot electric cord. I also borrowed an emergency 110-volt storm-drain pump from somebody at the boatyard. And I had a good-sized 110-volt transfer pump with green garden hoses connected and ready to go. Plus an empty five-gallon bucket at the ready. The inside of the boat looked like an industrial ER.

I had taken off work at noon and buzzed over to the marina to make last-minute tinkerings before the launch. The big old Travelift already sat astride LILIBET, and I knew we were going in today. The golf carts whizzed back and forth from the barns to the ramp. People called out encouragement. Chip talked about getting his swimming suit on.

When I flipped the on switch for the bilge pump, nothing happened. I knew juice was going somewhere, but nothing I did would activate that pump. The afternoon was passing, and I decided to rely on the 110-volt pumps. If three weren't enough then perhaps she was meant to sink. Besides, there wasn't a lot of water between my keel and the river bottom, so she couldn't go far if she sank. I climbed down the ladder, cleared away my winter worktable and toolbox, piled the tarps and work junk off to the side, and gave the boys the nod. Instantly they went to work. In minutes the Travelift snorted loudly, and the hydraulics raised

The Travelift at Watchamajig Boatyard brings LILIBET off her cradle for the Spring 2003 launch

the boat up in the air as high as it would go. People gathered round and followed the lift as it wheeled down the tar road to the launch ramp. I drove the pick up truck ahead and snapped photos.

I held my breath as the Travelift turned onto the ramp. This was exactly why Georgia had opted to miss the action. Too much anxiety. As the lift crept down the ramp with LILIBET's aft end first, Chip looked at his helpers and said, "She's heavy." They immediately hooked up two big cables to an army-surplus tow truck parked up on flat land and held the brakes on as the lift inched down the ramp. The keel touched the Mississippi River. It eased under water as the lift wheels met the river, too. Slowly, the hull began to disappear into the brown water, as did the legs of the lift. Soon, the beam supporting the lift engine reached water level. The slings still held LILIBET off the bottom. No one could tell how much depth lay between the keel bottom and the underwater ramp. There was about 18 inches of red bottom paint still showing above the water.

Chip looked at me and in a voice of amused authority asked, "Are you sure you want to go in?" I tried to look cool and nodded in the affirmative. "Yep," I replied.

At this point the placement of the slings, done when they picked the boat up from its cradle, became central to the operation. It seemed like a small thing, but by placing the straps farther forward on the hull than normal, there was enough swing backward when they lifted the after end at this moment to reach her out a little more than if she went straight down. It was ever so slight, but darned if that wasn't good thinking by the yard guys—in whom, until now, I had had less than great faith. Just then Chip announced, "She's floating." He could feel the relief of tension on the big yellow straps.

Jerry from Florida jumped on board and hurried through the hatch to check for leaks. We had plugged in the shore power a few minutes earlier. My big sump pump sat in the bilge next to the dead 12-volt bilge pump. I followed Jerry and found him up forward in the boat. Water was spurting in through several seams that I could have sworn were tight up on shore. A river had formed and was flowing over the floor frames toward the pumps under the Perkins diesel engine, which is the lowest part of the hull. I had hooked an inch-and-a-half plastic hose to the sump pump before we went in, and it filled dramatically with river water as the float valve keyed the electric motor. I heard someone outside say, "She's pumping." I was a little at a loss as to what really to do, but when the pump started pushing air through the pipe, I felt relieved. Jerry pointed out that the pump was keeping up so we weren't sinking, and if I had some cotton I should jam it into the leaking seams. I didn't of course—though I'll never be without it again—but good neighbor Pam, who was living on her boat ashore while she rebuilt, got me a salad bowl full of unspun cotton. I grabbed up a little screwdriver and started jamming cotton into the leaking seams.

Talk about a super-quick cure. Cotton swells when it gets wet—that's why cotton strands are used to caulk wooden boats from the outside when they're in the yard. Within minutes things had improved considerably, except where one seam was hiding behind the bilge stringer. There was also water coming from other hidden sources, but the pump was doing fine keeping up with it. No water had reached the top of the belly tank on which we were standing and in fact stayed well below it.

Clark, the wooden boat guy showed up to let me know that, "Hey, she's floating," a fact that I was critically aware of, but what the heck, affirmation is good. I asked him for a consultation on the hidden leaks, and he assessed the flow. "Don't worry for 48 hours," he said. "This is a really well-built boat. The wood will swell up tight by then. You'll see." And it did.

The yard guys tied LILIBET to the gas dock at the end of

LILIBET meets the Mississippi River after an arduous trip down the launch ramp, St. Paul, Spring 2003

the ramp so she'd be quickly accessible if things went south. The crowd wandered off, and I started to clean up the former industrial ER. By 7 p.m. the leaks were slowing considerably. I stowed the extra pumps and took a break to survey my new position.

LILIBET looked super on the water. My double boottop was exactly in the right place, and the black hull reflected the setting sun like a postcard. Clark the expert and Pam and a few other folks came down the ramp with champagne and plastic cups. We sat on the trunk cabin and toasted LILIBET, the boatyard, and the whole wooden boat scene. I called home and left a message for Georgia, letting her know it was a successful afternoon. I stayed aboard until 3 a.m. watching the water pump and enjoying the moonlight on the Mississippi and my neat little yacht. Perhaps I might become a ragbagger after all.

By midweek, the yard guys had hauled LILIBET away from the gas dock and moored her in a slip in the middle of a houseboat squadron parked side by side down the docks. My neighbors bore names like NAUGHTY-GULL and THE REAL LIFE. Okay.

The work routine we had established took a deep breath, and for a minute there we had to fight the urge to think of it as a done project. We got to know our immediate neighbors in their boxy houseboats. They all considered us a unique addition to the docks, and a couple of the elder

Floating at last. At the dock on the Mississippi River in St. Paul after the lauch, Spring 2003

boys liked to stop and visit with Georgia while she sanded and varnished. I was reluctant to start the power saws and sanders here in this peaceful little lagoon, but the marina had assured me it was all right, and when I apologized in advance to the boaters next to me, they claimed no problem. I bet they regretted that after a weekend or two of our presence, but no one said anything. I take that back. There was one loudspeaker announcement early on from a distant flybridge across the pond that reminded the world about no power tools being used on weekends. We kept right on going.

A Good Summer

Summer was kind to us in the weather department. Not a Saturday or a Sunday of rain from July through August, so progress was good. We established a nice work routine, hoping to be at a place by fall where we could say the project was in control. I worked below on the saloon cabinetry. It was picky, tedious work, with lots of starts and stops, and the amount of wood that was hauled down the dock for the job seemed enormous. I kept thinking that I would see the boat start to list as I continued building. I began on the starboard side of the saloon first, for no good reason other than I think I just wanted to put off remodeling the area of the galley sink and stove until I finalized the design in my head.

The first step was to anchor the new fuel tank in place and build it in. A million screws later, and with several miles of oak corner trim laid in place, the tank had a settee over it, followed by a chart table tied into the new angled-aft seating area. Sounds simple, but everything had to be fitted, cut, refitted, trimmed, sanded, painted or stained and varnished—and all the tops had to be removable so you could still get inside to string wires and hoses for the various systems as they were installed. New oak panels over the bulkheads followed, with oak vents to allow the boat a little breathing flow from bilge to cabin top. I reinstalled the old saloon shelf that runs just above the settee. It added some antique charm without overkill. I used part of the original saloon table as the chart tabletop.

It was a particularly hot summer, so my work costume while working in the cabin confines consisted of skimpy shorts. It was like a sauna. I probably lost a bit of winter blubber in the deal. I felt a little timid at first, sawing away with a saber saw or buzzing off trim corners with an angle grinder while I had so much skin exposed, but I soon got used to it. Aside from a blackened toenail where a cutoff board dropped on my bare feet and a slight swirl mark on my midriff from the angle grinder, things went pretty well. Mahogany panels for the new engine instruments and the AC panel box were added, and bit by bit the starboard side was complete.

The galley would go on the port side, so I installed the old propane two-burner stove and a new sink and counter top. Wow! This could turn out okay after all.

While I did this, Georgia stripped and refinished the miles of brightwork topside. She was a real sun devil, and her back soon turned the color of the wood she worked on. With her long silver hair and her sunglasses she was quite a flashy figure; no wonder the old boys liked to stop and chat. I took a break on an especially hot Sunday in August to help

The finished interior at the aft end of the main cabin

her refinish the inside of the gunwales. By 2 o'clock I was nearly overcome with heat exhaustion or sunstroke or maybe both, and watched in awe as Georgia just kept on blazing away at that railing.

I wasn't alone. As the days went by, our neighbors all managed to comment about her amazing work capacity and stick-to-it mindset. The history of women and boat projects as a sensitive mix was certainly on their minds, and when she didn't throw up her hands and scream, "I quit," they all shook their heads in disbelief. (Just between you and me, she did whisper it once or twice.)

About this time—better late than never—we decided it might be nice to have a sunshade. Closing the boat up tightly every week invites summer mold and, of course, wood rot. Also, the heat made us worry about the cabin tops and our own health. Georgia had a roll of black cherry Sunbrella, earmarked for the sail covers, but since we wouldn't be stepping the mast till next spring, it was cut and sewn into a nice big rectangle, with tags and grommets spaced along the edges. I built a temporary mast from 2 x 4s; it was inserted into the maststep at the forward part of the trunk cabin and extended up through the cabin top to the height of the boom gallows back of the cockpit. We hoisted the boom into place and fastened the gooseneck to the top of the temporary mast stub. The framework was instantly painted white, and next day I installed the new sunshade/rainshade over the boom using black elastic bungees to catch the lifeline stanchions at their bases. It was spectacular. Everyone on the dock said we had just invented sliced bread. Now we could leave the boat open and not worry about moisture.

At this point we had a surprise visit from our friends, the architect sculptor and his wife, plus their dog. It was a sunny Sunday afternoon, and they just appeared there on the dock. For a moment I was nervous that my interior design and carpentry work would come under fire, but as it turned out they were very complimentary, and the guilt feelings that had lingered (remember, this is Minnesota), disappeared.

It was a good summer. And it was, for us, perhaps the speediest summer of our lives. Aside from a high school reunion in Eau Claire, Wisconsin—Georgia's fortieth—and the annual family picnic up at Blue Lake, we never missed a weekend of work on the boat. We became part of the regular weekend marina gang, and it was fun. I also usually spent a few long evenings every week after work at the boat, driving from the western suburbs over to St. Paul so I could fit a few boards or trim some edges on the interior. By the end of August things were really looking good. Even my interior design/construction, which was always a thing of unilateral doubt, began to get the nod.

Water levels on the Mississippi, however, went to their lowest point in years. No rain and the constant flow of river water down the drain made our docks sink lower and lower into the surrounding landscape. I had no depthfinder hooked up, and I was too chicken to use a long stick to find the bottom, so every Saturday morning and on my weeknight visits I expected to see LILIBET lying against the dock with the decks tilted. It had to be close, but every time I arrived at the boat, even with still no rain, LILIBET remained free floating. I didn't want to think about the pullout coming in October.

In the last week of August, I scheduled the boatyard to rewire and fire up the engine. I wanted to cruise her around the marina before we hauled her out for the winter. The wiring was a project that had been on my list since I first stepped aboard, and now was the time. As I had worked on the interior over the past year, it became clear how really screwy the old systems were. I'm sure they worked for the former owners—and they did get across the ocean, so there's something to be said there—but boy oh boy this stuff was a mess. It's just not in my bones, however, to know how Franklin's lightning goes through a bunch of wires the right way, the wrong way, alternating, directly, grounded, single phase, 110-, 220- or 12-volt, red wires, green wires, black or white ones.

An e-mail from the former owner had mentioned that he and his partner had rewired the boat at some point in the past several years, but looking closely at the result made me wonder further as to how she had survived their good intentions—even though I'm sure it all made perfect sense to them. A pencil-drawn wiring diagram found in a plastic garbage bag in the forepeak didn't exactly cure my doubts. Still—and this is important—ragging on someone else's systems aside, now would be the time to make it very clear that it was the lads from England who brought LILIBET across the ocean and kept her floating through fair weather and foul. It had to be quite a feat—and one I will never attempt—so a few bad strands of wire and some ill housekeeping really don't figure into a whole lot of productive thinking. My apologies, boys. (But she was quite a mess.)

Knowing when to let go is a good thing. So I was thinking that while the time might come for me to become user friendly with the little Perkins diesel, in the electronics department it was perhaps time to find another expert. An electrician. My choices were fairly clear, if slightly limited. On the one hand Georgia had a cousin who had been an electrician all his life, and he had a son who was the same. They were big, robust, nice guys with a can-do attitude and a pair of pliers. They offered to come on down to the marina and wire her up. On the other hand Chip, the marina guy, said he could do it, too.

I had had almost a year to think about it while I worked inside the hull. The family idea was appealing because of the obvious savings in cash and the good fellowship of family help. The down side was that these boys have north woods cabins and kids and grandkids, and after a long week at work, plenty of goofing off to do. I'm pretty sure they didn't realize the time and complexity involved here. Also, a house is different from a boat in a lot of ways, wiring being one of them. I am certainly not suggesting that a boat is more difficult, more technical, more sophisticated, trickier, better, or nothing like that, you see. Just different.

The worrisome concept of using the local marina was the cast of characters. My recent fuel-tank episode with this same group had given me pause. It's true that boat service departments can be frustrating, but this one was a country of its own. You sign up to get some work done, and then you wait. If you make some noise, you wait longer. Most of my neighbors at the marina were grudgingly used to this system. On the upside, at least the yard boys and their tools were at the marina and their livelihoods did seem to depend on doing boat work. The dicey part was that most if not all of the shop guys lived at the marina, so in some ways we boat owners were sort of seen as guests in their homes— even though we paid for the privilege.

After spending lots of time working on LILIBET at odd hours, I got a fix on the routine around the yard. After business hours, it did resemble a little backwoods town of sorts. Chip, the yard boss, was sort of the mayor, and everyone else deferred to him. He was a big, sort of rough character in his 40s who tended to communicate in short, garbled, tough-guy sentences. He drove a pickup truck during the day and rode a motorcycle around the yard after work. He had a black lab dog who took handouts but didn't say thank you, and his ex-wife ran the marina store and lived in a houseboat on the shore next to the store. Chip and his current squeeze lived aboard his boat on one of the docks, and he was the proprietor of his own marine service business within the marina itself, so that helps explain the independent nature of things.

Chip hired a crew of likewise rough, live-in characters on a job-to-job basis who all seem to be sort of good at some part of the marine service industry. Marty the welder, who made my stainless-steel tanks (and a pretty good job of it too), lived in a run down Chris-Craft hull under a plastic tarp with his cat. Every so often he would lose track of the cat and blame Jerry from Florida for somehow torturing and killing his beloved pet. In fact the cat was over in the woods doing his own little murders and would soon return home. But until then, Marty and Jerry would go at it for hours on end—the one shouting tearful accusations, the other roaring across the pond that he didn't hurt the damned cat!

Another guy was good with engines (not diesels), and someone else was a pretty fair painter. There was a guy with silver hair and a salty complexion who drove the Travelift and the big yard trucks, moving boats in and out of the water and rearranging them in rows along the driveway. He never said much; if he wasn't on some machine, roaring along the riverfront, he seemed to be nonexistent. Several other members of the team drifted around from pillar to post doing odd jobs. Mostly everyone drifted from one end of the marina to the other and back again, sometimes stopping midway to hang out with some of the other live-in boat folks who forever seemed to be in the middle of their own restoration projects. (Is there any question now why the true woody marinas are few and far between?)

Time was running out on my making a decision about the electrical job. I decided to go with Chip the marina guy.

Complex and involved are surely the nicest words I can apply to this wiring project. The correct term on so many levels might be closer to "damned difficult." Agreeing to do the work is one thing; actually doing it and then completing the job is a horse of a different color, as I should have known—actually I did know but thought I'd risk the chance of smooth sailing.

For those who are used to working on houseboats, the Spartan dictates of my old sailboat made for some alarming times. The yard guys here are big. Just the idea of their clomping on board with those size-12 work boots and fooling around in the wiring department made me fearful. I took a three-day vacation from work to get things started—kind of explain the things I needed, the costs, the schedule, the finish date. I was cautiously optimistic as I drove over to the marina to meet Chip, the electrical wizard. He didn't show up. No one knew where he was. For the first two days, my guy was absent from the marina. On the third day he showed up with a tiny red toolbox and listened to me for 15 minutes while he looked vacantly around the saloon. Finally he said, "Okay, I'll start on it right away."

That was a Friday. My interior reconstruction was put to a stop in preparation for the wiring and engine work ahead. I drove over every night after work to check progress.

In the first week, a couple of tool boxes showed up, and all the loose panels I had built were stacked here and there, leaving the engine and the ribs exposed. No other sign of progress. In the second week, on Monday, there was a joint decision, somehow going past me—not too well thought out—to disconnect the old hydraulic system. Because of the rat's-nest condition of the entire electromechanical system, the only ones who would know for sure what worked and what didn't would be the former owners, who were in

England and rather unreachable. By all appearances the hydraulic system was pretty far gone anyway, but the lines were plumbed for the anchor windlass. The old windlass was a monster—a pretty one, but still a real clunker—and certainly not original, so I was bound to find an electric rig that had some charm. It would be a project replacing the old one, but that was my deal.

Jerry cut the hydraulic lines, and they immediately bled into the bilge. Whatever else the hydraulics ran besides the anchor windlass was now inoperable. The steering was mechanical—cable, rudder to wheel post—so that was okay. What else, I didn't know, but perhaps the philosophy was that one is better stripping out the unknown old and going new when the need arose. We would see.

In the third week, a hot-water heater, a new bilge pump, and a freshwater pump showed up, along with a roll of wire. We were now at the last part of September, haulout was getting closer, the project was dragging, and I started getting steamed. Some of my dock neighbors allowed that this was standard procedure with this marina, and I allowed that, yes, this was the same routine as the fuel-tank episode. I decided to make some waves.

I found Chip and the liveaboard gang lounging around behind some old boat hulls having a few beers. It looked like a hobo gathering. He knew he was in for it, so he made nice, and after a few heated paragraphs I decided to quit while I was ahead. He agreed to "get stroking," and I left the yard. The rest of the gang glared after me as if I were an unreasonable twit and wouldn't speak to me for the standard three-day period.

*   *   *

I gave it three days and drove over to the yard one night after work to see what was getting done. All was quiet along the long driveway down to the docks. I felt a gathering sense of dread as I climbed aboard and descended into the dark cabin. There was my AC panel box, looking good. Instead of spending $500 on a new AC breaker panel, I had salvaged the one that was on the boat when I bought her. I had mounted it on a refinished mahogany cabinet door from up forward, and a new red wire was neatly tied into this box, looking for all the world like someone knew what they were doing. I snooped into the bilge. Water lines were connected to the hot-water heater and new fuel lines were hooked up to the new stainless-steel fuel tanks. My nice new "Chesapeake Series" engine gauges, also mounted on a mahogany panel, were wired, and the new bilge pump seemed to be connected. The freshwater pump was screwed down to a plywood board anchored under a seat cover and had red wires leading off to somewhere. Progress. Still, I couldn't leave the marina without checking in with Chip. It's good to be encouraging, and any communication is better than assumptions.

Chip lived on his boat over on another dock. His boat was one of the many works in progress at the marina. It was a cabin cruiser with a big chip in the nose where someone drove into her one night. He kept it mostly covered with blue canvas that flapped around in the wind; he also kept the windows covered with black shades. His boat was surrounded by broken-down houseboats belonging to his pals, so it was a little like visiting the dogpatch section when you went there. You knock on the hull and he scuffles up to the canvas entry flap, looks out, and says, "Yeaahh?" This time he invited me in.

On the weirdorama scale, which goes to ten, this deal read at least twenty-four. I mean, these guys were all in their 40s, so chalking them up as kids just didn't cut it. Inside, the boat was not a boat at all, but a really small South St. Paul tavern/cabin/lounge. In a nine- by twelve-foot space with six-foot ceilings, there was an old, giant, floor-model television with plastic-laminate simulated-wood veneer peeling off, two careworn couches, a floor lamp, a motel-style coffee table, three or four area rugs the color of dirt, piles of magazines, ash trays, unwashed dishes, empty and half-empty booze bottles, a big bowl of dog food, a big, black dog, and a corner galley setup hiding under blackened pots and pans. Since it was a little chilly outside, the heat was on full blast, and with the room full of unwashed big-boy bodies wearing work clothes, things got dicey fast. They were all scrunched together drinking and watching TV. I knew I was among unfriendlies as I walked down the steps into the cabin.

Jerry, wearing his black baseball cap trimmed with red and orange flames and his blue/green sunglasses, was ready to rumble—even though I was a customer paying $60 per hour of his time. I decided to be careful. I put on my innocent look, apologized for interrupting, and squeezed my buns into the corner of a couch.

"Looks like we're making progress over there," I ventured optimistically. "How's it going?"

Chip jumped in, explaining that somebody's relative died, parts were on back order, an emergency job had popped up, someone else got sick. Otherwise everything was going good. "Why do you ask?"

"Oh, ya know," I said, "I'm gonna put her back on land in a couple of weeks, and I've still got tons of work to do on her. I need my boat back so I can finish."

No reaction.

Jerry ticked off a list of what he had done and so did Chris. It was a lot of not much, but then what did I know? I answered a few questions about stuff that was in question. I got ready to leave. We all grinned and nodded. I asked when they thought they might be done, but got no real answer. I asked for a ballpark on what the charges were by now. Sideways looks. "Gotta adderallup." I found my way out.

"Gosh," I said to myself on the drive home, "that went well."

Who knows? Maybe running a marine repair business is really a mind bender. All those nuts and bolts to think about. Which goes where?

Fall Projects

A week later, I drove over from work on a Friday night to check the scene. This was into the first week of October, and almost six weeks into what even I knew should have been a one-week project. Jerry was skulking along the driveway. The weather was getting chilly, and he had traded his sandals for a really bad pair of gym shoes. I rolled up next to him and stopped the truck. He was defensive about progress, so I decided to move along. In parting, he let me know that these rush jobs were really an inconvenience and bringing a weird boat like that one to St. Paul was a goofy idea anyway. I said, "Yer right about that," and rolled down the road to where the boat was docked.

After looking around the dim cabin, it was clear that some work was being done, because the clutter of cardboard boxes and parts wrappers had grown, along with empty soda bottles, rags, wire clippings, and cigarette butts. I had kept a pretty good mental picture of the things I needed the yard guys to accomplish, and I could see that slowly stuff was happening along the planned concept of a new wiring harness. Maybe by next June it all might be finished. The freshwater system was working to some degree, but because LILIBET is a sailboat with two-thirds of her body under water, there isn't a whole lot of distance from the sink drain to the actual pond level outside. Before we launched, I installed a drain shutoff valve just above the through-hull fitting so water wouldn't back up into the sink when we were cruising along with the portside rail at sea level.

Jerry had run some water into the sink, and now it just sat there sloshing around. He had mentioned that he didn't understand the drain shutoff valve setup, so I should check it out and let him know what was what. I switched on a clamp-on light and peered under the sink. Hmmm. Jerry had used a straight piece of high-pressure rubber water pipe to connect the sink drain to the drain pipe going through the hull, and it was stiff as a board. It started at my new shutoff valve, just above the through-hull fitting, under the new aft seating modules and ran diagonally up under the sink to the sink drain pipe. This hose needed to make a sixty-degree or so angle just under the sink, so water could run downhill to the outside world. Normally, one would buy an angle piece from a plumbing supplier and use water hose clamps to hold it in place. Jerry had simply muscled this ultra-stiff pressure hose onto the sink drain, making the hose crimp at the bend and forcing the sink to pop loose from the cabinet fastenings holding it down. The upward pressure had also caused the sink to take part of the Formica countertop along with it. On the other end of the rubber pipe, the pressure caused the connection at my new shutoff valve to leak, and water from the sink was dripping slowly into the bilge.

*   *   *

"Red Hell and Black Death!" as someone in the British Navy used to say. I closed the cabin doors, penned a note saying not to touch the boat until we talked, and drove home. I looked up Chip next morning and suggested that perhaps he assign other work to the man from Florida. Trying to be politic, and knowing that these same guys would be in charge of the soon-to-come haulout, I tried to downplay my need to push someone off the dock. Besides, they were all younger and in a whole lot better shape than I was. I asked him not to say anything to Jerry, who was a really sweet guy, but just keep him off my boat. Well, of course no one waved at me any more when I drove past the barns—especially Jerry from Florida, but hey, I might still be a stinkpotter at heart, and bad manners are just part of that scene. Still, I couldn't for the life of me feel guilty about my reaction to someone screwing up my boat.

On the following Saturday I cleaned off all the garbage and replaced everything as it was before the project started, and took stock of the situation. I had decided that I myself would redo the water hookup after the boat was ashore. No big deal. The remaining wiring was up to Chip, although I doubted he would ever finish the job. I would either pay him for what he had done so far, and get someone else to finish, or get him to finish the job after she went ashore. There just wasn't that much work left to do. The bad Formica would have to be replaced. What a pain.

The next day, Sunday, the marina was very quiet. The lads were not in sight and things on board looked back to normal. In the course of our conversation the day before,

Chip had said he had finally gotten the engine started. I found out later he did it by shooting some compressed ether starting spray into it, a total no-no for diesels. I wanted to run her a little before she came out for the winter.

I turned on some of the new switches and cranked her over. After a few false starts, the little Perkins rumbled to life and big billows of blue smoke belched out of the exhaust port. I had opened the throttle a little too much while she was cranking. As the engine rid itself of my overdose of diesel fuel, the smoke cleared away and the boat sat at the dock talking away as if it were making up for lost time. What a great feeling to hear that nice, rich growl down there beneath the decks. The pond was flat calm; there was no wind. Georgia and I decided to back her into the channel and see how she handled. The plan was to back straight out—not even all the way out—and then bring her straight back in just to see how she responded to the shift from forward to reverse. Then, as old people will do, we decided to complicate things just a little by keeping a bowline on her; Georgia would stay on the dock to pull her back in if necessary. Okay.

Well, that seemed like a good idea. But then we complicated things just a tiny bit more by deciding to keep a stern line on her, too, and Georgia would act as the pivot control, leading both lines out and taking them back in at the same time as the boat maneuvered in and out of the dock. These lines also had to be fed loosely around several cleats on the dock so as not to fall into the water and become fouled on dock legs or our propeller. Hmmmm.

Well, the idea was that never having tested her before,

we just didn't want to go crashing into the line of boats parked behind us. That seemed rightly Minnesota prudent. So Georgia gave the signal that she was ready, and off we went with a ginger little shift into reverse and the boat obediently moved back.

For a couple of seconds there, things looked hunky-dory. But then the bowline feeding out started to go taut as it hung up on one of the cleats. I eased the controls into forward, but the engine was just idling and couldn't produce the needed forward motion. (Remember, LILIBET's prop is a little two-blade zinger measuring about a foot from tip to tip.) Nothing quick happens at idle speed. In fact nothing happens. We ran out of bowline, and the taut rope pulled our bow toward the dock while the stern, still on a loose line, moved away from the dock and headed toward a nice fiberglass powerboat with a "For Sale" sign on it. Georgia was busy loosening the snaggle on the bowline and had to double back fast to haul in the stern. It's a hard pull, because you're trying to drag that big keel blade sideways through the water. She did it, though, and finally we were back dockside. Adding a few revisions to the ropes and pulley system, we tried again with roughly the same amount of success. A little frustrating and embarrassing, but I was beginning to get a fix on what the steerage and deadweight carry was like in docking. Another try or two, and I could tell that the trick on this thing was plenty of practice and knowing when to goose the engine and when to back her off. It's similar to docking a powerboat, but much more tender. The old law of "Too much dorking around in close quarters causes trouble" came back to me in a hurry.

We took a break, tried a time or two more, and then I noticed the smell of burnt oil. Glancing into the cabin, I could see this blue cloud that had gathered there, and I hurried below to hit the kill switch. Thankfully, we were still at the dock. I opened the engine box and saw immediately that one of the fuel injectors was loose where it was bolted onto the engine head. Black oil was bubbling out and dripping down onto the hot manifold. The place reeked of burnt oil. I left the engine box open so things could cool down, and with much discussion of spring lines and looseness and tightness and this and that, we tied LILIBET back into place and sat down on the cabin roof.

Deck caulking. Now these are two words that strike fear in the heart of many a poor boat boy. Every book I've read about the repair and maintenance of wooden boats (and my library grows like kudzu) either omits the onerous process altogether, or briefly refers to it as something left to professionals, or gives us a short paragraph starting with "The trouble with teak" and ending with "might be better to fiberglass over it." For lots of folks that might be true.

Someone had laid glass over plywood on the deck of my second boat, DENALI. It was easy to take care of and didn't leak—so there. For some of us, however, the look of that beautiful sprung planking curving its way around the trunk cabin and wedging into the bow in perfect order just can't be given up easily. The teak deck on LILIBET was leaking when I bought her, and the survey mentioned a need for recaulking. In fact a redecking wouldn't be a bad plan, since the existing teak was worn down pretty good. What to do?

With all the other stuff going on, and still trying to hold down a job to pay for it, I decided as a first measure of action to recaulk the teak and seal it. I know. Some would point out the true classic beauty of bare gray teak glowing under the moon. So free, so simple, so photogenic, so easy on the feet. Sealing teak is a dumb idea, they would say, because it forever darkens the wood, and more importantly, teak is a grainy sort of wood that tends to flake off naturally. So you have to continuously reseal and reseal. Perhaps. And that's okay for "newish" teak, with everything absolutely perfect—but we all know it won't last. One day, it will inevitably end up with wear ridges in the wood, screw heads peeking through, stains from fish guts and boat food, crumbled caulking, and leaks whose source you can't locate. Most people will then tear off the teak and replace it with canvas or glass. I guess I was just not ready for that.

We started on the after deck and began the learning process. While I dithered on some last-minute interior reconstruction before the big wiring project, Georgia started ripping out the old caulking from between the deck seams. She used a screwdriver, a wire brush, and a paint-stripping pad to do the job. Driving the flat screwdriver blade along the joint ripped up the old caulking, wire brushing took out most of the old snags left behind, and scrubbing along the nearly clean joints removed the remaining old particles. A shop vac was used to suck up all the dirt.

The next step was to drizzle a liquid wood hardener into the open seams using a two-inch paintbrush. We saw the liquid hardener drain down into several areas that had opened up under the old caulk. These areas were doused thoroughly with the hope that the excess liquid would follow the same path that had formerly allowed water entry. Wood hardener is aggressive stuff. It discolors and penetrates anything it touches and one has to be careful about spills. Think of it as similar to the alien goo that dripped down through the steel plates of the space ship in the movie *Aliens*. Once the hardener was dry, we taped with blue mastic tape the edges of all the seams we had cleaned out so far, and then we were ready to caulk.

Filling the seams with tube caulk is tedious, slow, and uncomfortable work. The caulk is black and very sticky. I ran the tube along the cleaned-out joints, squeezing in just enough caulk to fill the trenches, all the while hoping this was the correct approach. I did it in short stints, because I didn't want the fresh caulk to "skin up" and make removing the tape a nightmarish hell—which it is anyway. Before I pulled the tape, I used a flat, plastic paste spreader cut to about an inch wide to run a smoothing pass over the filled joints. This picked up excess caulk and left a flat, smooth surface in the grooves. The secret is to never make a second swipe over that nice, smooth surface, as it inevitably results in making things look like a freshly plowed field.

Tape removal is picky and cautious work, because you are never in a comfortable position so it is hard on your knees and your back. Also, the tape comes up in unpredictable lengths—depending on how even you made the lengths and how much you overlapped—and brings with it all the extra caulk left over from the smoothing process. When you pick up the tape, it curls around on itself and your fingers, making your hands black and sticky. A good throwaway rag or two is important. Generally, I used a plastic bucket to drop the tape into as it came off the deck. If there is any breeze, however, the tape likes to fly around, coming to rest and sticking on nice varnished trim work, railings, and your clothing, so caution and focus are very important. After the tape was removed, we let the caulk cure for a few days before shuffling around on it. So much for the mysteries of deck caulking. If it all falls out by the end of next summer, I'll consult the experts.

Fall 2003 found me and the yard guys at an impasse. I finally came to the conclusion that not everyone was going to be as driven as I was about my boat project, and these guys had far too much lying about to do to accommodate my ambitious schedule. Ten days after the aborted cruise around the marina, I begged off work on a Thursday and showed up to help get LILIBET roped around to the gas dock and back up the ramp to shore. I stayed on board with a helper from the marina staff while Chip fired up his little orange towboat. We roped LILIBET out of the slot and got her just about turned into the channel before the towboat's engine died, leaving us drifting backward into a raft of houseboats tied to the dock behind us. The helper and I frantically fended off as the towboat finally came back to life and jerked us out of harm's way. This happened several times more on our little trip around the marina to the haulout ramp. Start, stop, drift, crash. No major harm done to anyone, and eventually we headed in at the ramp. Once there, to no one's great surprise, we suddenly stopped about two boat lengths from where we wanted to be. Aground. Lightly aground, but still aground. The river was, indeed, very low this year.

The yard guys tied her nose with a long rope to a truck on the ramp. I made sure the rope was secure on the stout old anchor windlass so we wouldn't pull something loose from the boat. Reasoning had it that there was at least two feet of sand and mud under us before bedrock. After poking around with a long pole, we figured that LILIBET was hung up on a ridge with a little deeper water just in front of her nose. The driver backed up, and we were dragged a ways further in to shore. I could feel the grinding of soil under the hull and could only trust to luck that we weren't dragging the lumber off the lead keel. This was our darkest hour. The idea was to get us in far enough for the Travelift to connect straps and pull her out. The Travelift was our only option: there was no place to put a crane, and the choices of action beyond floating down the Mississippi to somewhere below the Mason-Dixon Line were just about nil.

The tow rope from the truck broke, as tow ropes will, and they attached a heavy braided-nylon hawser to my windlass. More pulling. Suddenly LILIBET cleared whatever mound of gravel and mud had stopped us, and floated free just as the truck did another back-up pull. We lurched forward with me yelling STOP, and hit the concrete ramp under our bow with an abrupt shudder.

Chip bailed out at this point. He no doubt didn't want to be involved in any disasters while I still owed him money, and I was left standing alone on the deck of my stranded sailboat. About a half hour later a new gang arrived, including the marina manager dressed in a wet suit for diving. The Travelift came down the ramp and went in so far that the driver, standing on a platform that was six feet off the ground, had to take off his shoes because he was standing in water up to his ankles. The lower part of the lift's engine block was under water, and we were still a little too far out to get the straps on her. Kevin, the marina manager, swam around the hull trying to figure out what to do. I stood on the deck and held my breath.

It was decided that we would attach the straps at an angle as far back on the hull as we could and raise her up, hoping to slingshot her forward enough to get her under the Travelift. It worked, but because she was now resting part way on the bottom of the river and part way on the ramp, with about a foot of bottom paint showing, the hull began to roll sideways. I scrambled to the high side of the deck and really held my breath. They relocated the front strap a little farther back along the hull, and when I determined there was nothing else they could do, gave them the okay to lift her out. Out she came, cocked at a crazy angle with her bow down, her stern up, and the decks slanting dramatically to starboard. The Travelift inched up the ramp and up the drive—a slow process—to the same spot where LILIBET had been laid up last year. This time I asked the yard guys to position her so the bow was pointing toward the river, which they did. They blocked her up, gave her a power wash, and took off for lunch.

*   *   *

Chip showed up with his bill for wiring and water system and a rebuilt alternator and much more, which I agreed to pay in full. The bill was for parts and labor to this point in the project, without further rancor and with a promise to finish the job at some future time, which we both knew wouldn't happen. The haulout was a four-hour project. Everyone was pooped, including me. I inspected the bottom for damage, found only minor scrapes, and went home.

That weekend I painted below the waterline with the same red copper as in the spring, and Georgia and I continued to reef out the deck joints. The temperature hit the sixties. The sky was bright blue. The leaves along the river bluffs blazed away: gold, red, yellow. The first year of ragbag endeavor was complete. We would return before snowfall to continue building, do more deck work, and finally batten her down for the winter.

In retrospect, this had been a remarkably productive year. The old girl was tight, and the exterior was near completion. The interior was well on its way to being presentable, though a lot remained to be done. Wiring was still a biggie, and of course the injector leak had to be taken care of. Strangely, Chip had installed a new/rebuilt alternator but had never hooked it up. Having some failed alternator experience from my youth, I knew its main purpose in life was to charge the batteries to keep the 12-volt system breathing. This was especially important, since I had just replaced the old batteries with two marine 12-volters and a big double-sized Goliath to power the house and lights. The big battery was not hooked up, of course, but the two 12-volters were. They cranked the engine famously, and I needed the alternator hooked in to keep them doing that. Somehow I would get the wiring done and the injector leak fixed before spring. The real task at hand now lay in finding a more suitable water home for this boat and then getting her mast up and rigged.

November 2003 came and went. We bought all new blue plastic and tarped the boat for winter using the boom as our horizontal tent pole and tightly lacing up the bow and stern. What a difference from the previous year. No odd building of plastic pipes and zip ties, and plenty of room to climb aboard and stand up in the cockpit. A huge improvement. I returned regularly to check the cover and plug our newly wired shore-power cord into the barnyard electrical circuits to trickle-charge the batteries with my new charger. Cool! I rigged a positive and negative leg to the giant new battery, and when I switched on the charger, its little red and green trickle charge light came on, so God bless us, we'll keep our fingers crossed for the winter.

A Second Winter

The boatyard mechanics never did finish the wiring job nor did they repair the leaky injector. They just stopped work on my boat and went to Florida for the winter. At first I got all confused and ticked off. In fact I was downright depressed for a couple of months. December was pretty bleak in the boat department, what with the cold weather, which pretty much puts the kibosh on projects on board, and little to bring to the studio this year for refinishing. Add to that the rough experience of our haulout, with no better prospects for future river ins and outs at this location. There were nights at home when we just didn't even refer to the old boat LILIBET.

Christmas came and went. By the end of February 2004, I could put in a little weekend time on the interior of the boat. I ditched the little electric fan heater I had been using and replaced it with a new hot-oil convection heater meant for warming that spare bedroom; it made a big difference.

I also made an executive electrical decision. I needed power to operate, and since the marina wingnuts were in Florida, they obviously had no need for their 30-amp plug box over there on the barn wall. It was the only box with

consistent power and was used to provide power to an old
plastic-tent-covered hulk in which one of the boys in past
years had lived—heaping with snow this time of year. The
old boat sat there deserted for the winter, plastic torn and
flapping in the wind. I waded through the knee-deep snow
drifts and unplugged the adapter connecting the old tub to
the power box. I waded over with it to my own yellow cord
and attached it. Wow! For a minute there I half expected
an alarm to go off, but nothing exciting happened except I
had the instant ability to run the lights, the battery charger,
the radio, the heater, and even some light weight power
tools without kicking off the breaker. Incredibly good for-
tune. After some indecision, I also decided to leave that
adapter plug on my boat when I left for the day. If I had
figured this deal out, so would plenty of other guys. To my
intense pleasure, no one ever inquired about the plug, and
by March, I was beginning to make a little progress
forward of the main saloon.

I had long ago decided to put a refrigerator on board
(some of my old stinkpotter ways just couldn't be thwarted,
I suppose). Just the thought of popping a cold one during
those hot summer afternoons made my eyes go wide whenever I passed the mini-refrigerator section at the building
supply store.

At this point, I should say something about certain
choices when it comes to restoring/refurbishing an old
boat—particularly an old sailboat. This is where the indi-
vidual character of the owner/designer/project director
(that would be me) comes out. Any sailor knows that a

110-volt anything besides cabin lights and a dockside radio-CD player doesn't rightly live on a sailboat. Especially on a classic antique historically significant special old wooden cruising yacht like LILIBET.

Most sailors would say that the eighteen by twenty inch by fourteen inches deep wooden ice box—painted gray on the inside, with a drain hole into the bilge, surrounded by good old-fashioned brown cork insulation and covered with a nice hinged oak board—would certainly be the aesthetically right thing to keep around. And I get their point. Ya know, throw in a bag of ice and some beers—maybe even a steak for the grill and don't sweat the small stuff—and someday it may come back to that. But the thing is that for the predictable future we're going to be inland-lake sailors. We're going to spend more time tied to the dock enjoying the view than under sail. We know this because having lived on our previous yacht, it's just the way things are on good-sized boats that aren't cruising the ocean—unless, of course, you're one of those manic personalities who can't stand to relax and must have constant toil and tearing to keep you happy. We're not.

In fact the whole point in having the boat in the first place, aside from the great restoration project itself, was to gain a place to spend weekends away from the city, relaxing with a book and a fishing rod—a little uncomplicated cooking, some dockside visiting, and, of course, a little sailing. Civilized camping out. And I might add, if you're ever (heaven forbid) thinking along these lines, the size of boat can be important. Many who like mostly to ram out of the harbor, hoist up the sails, tack and jibe like crazy, then slam back to the dock and disappear into the nearest shopping mall will choose a smaller, probably fiberglass, boat that needs little by way of steady maintenance, but also lacks the grand feeling of stretching out when you sleep.

So, back to the refrigerator. I installed one. It's a 110-volt one-quarter-scale white rectangle with reversible door hinges, a pint-sized freezer, nice wire racks to hold stuff, a drawer for veggies, and even an egg tray. When we're out on the water it goes quiet, and we keep a bag of ice in the cockpit for drinks. It stays in place even when LILIBET is rolling heavily by being built snugly into its little cubicle and by stout tie-downs across the door when we're sailing. Of course we don't load it up with heavy bottles and loose dishes of leftover food, as at home. When we're at the dock and plugged into shore power, it hums along, keeping things nice and cool. What small condensation there is drains into the bilge and eventually is pumped over the side. These days one can, of course, spend a lot of money on a 12-volt refrigerator that can operate at sea. We're not there yet.

In March as the temperature inched upward, I ripped out all the old cabinetry in the forward compartment and started framing up the new spaces. Slow going at first after a winter of being away from it, and of course the bloom was off the rose after a year of doing this kind of thing, but as time passed, a new groove began to form and I could see some progress. By April, I had the new white refrigerator in place on the starboard side just forward of the saloon and next to that a new, rather small storage cabinet, and forward of that all the way to the chain locker a big roomy raised sleeping platform with lift-up cover boards for access to the bilge. By May both the starboard and port sides were trimmed out with oak, stained, and painted, and I was heading back down the port side ready to attack the new head (that's sailor talk for bathroom).

To backtrack just a little: It should be noted that in February, as the end of winter poked its nose out from behind the snow drifts, I began to wake up at night worrying about the spring launching. My best hope, the Lake City Marina on Lake Pepin, did in fact turn me down because of LILIBET being wooden rather than fiberglass. No amount of good reasoning or downright pleading would change the verdict there, and I finally had to face that I might be driving three-plus hours in heavy Friday night traffic up to a mooring space in Duluth and putting up with the short season there, the bad weather, and the worse water conditions. One guy told me to be prepared for two kinds of water—dead flat or pounding waves and cold rain. Great.

Quite desperate, I put together several packets of photos showing LILIBET being launched in the river last year. They were good shots of the hull and the new black freeboard, and plenty showing off Georgia's brightwork efforts. I mailed these to the marinas on Lake Minnetonka out where I work. I didn't really expect any response, so it was a big surprise when I got telephone calls from first one and then a second one of the very yards that had initially turned me down (too big, too old, too wooden). Both marinas raved about the pictures—and sure, they'd love to have LILIBET at their docks. I was relieved and also feeling pretty okay about the work we had done on the old girl to get her to pass muster with this crowd.

A New Home

After some further talks and plans, I decided on the old Shorewood Yacht Club about 10 minutes from my office. John and his wife Judy own and operate the place, and they were most gracious about making us feel welcome. John grabbed his long bamboo dipstick, and we walked out to the end of dock #2, still slippery with ice patches. It was very early in the season, just into March by now, and here and there the lake ice was breaking up. John jammed the stick through the mushy surface, and we bent down anxiously, watching the little yellow foot markers as they disappeared into the cold water. Eight and a half feet, give or take a couple of inches. John rubbed his chin and guessed that if the coming season were to be dry, as it was last summer, LILIBET might be sitting in the mud by October next, but there should still be enough water to keep her standing upright. We cooked a deal, I got an end slot on the dock, and we set a date for bringing her in, May 27, 2004. Cross Country Transfer, the same movers that brought her from Annapolis, would haul her from St. Paul. The Shorewood Travelift would be too light to launch a boat the size of LILIBET, so we scheduled Rocket Crane Company to lift her in. I had never launched a boat with a crane and it seemed pretty scary, but the name Rocket gave me a feeling of marginal confidence.

Also, in February, my nice old studio building was purchased by a developer who planned to convert it into residential condominiums. This was predictable, since mine was one of the few buildings unclaimed by the hot real estate market in Minneapolis. All the tenants knew it was just a matter of time before notice was given. I had thirty days to remove seven years' worth of accumulation, including the boat stuff. Things started to hit the dumpster, and sailboat gear began to find its way into our apartment. Fat sail bags in Georgia's work room. Coils of standing rigging under the coffee table. Whisker poles in the hallway. Spreaders in a corner behind the television. A wind generator on a pole in my office room. A duffle bag full of running rigging behind the dining table. These bits and pieces, soon to be brought back onboard, remained constant reminders of the magnitude of our little restoration project throughout the later part of the winter.

April brought still warmer days, and with LILIBET's impending move from St. Paul to Shorewood, I had to get after the hull again. The cold and dry winter weather had opened planking seams, and some caulking was necessary to bring her back to being ready for the launch. I tried driving a few lines of cotton as described in the boat-repair books. It does take some practice. Determining how much cotton to use is difficult, as is deciding what to do when a seam has a lot of tight good caulk still in place. I mean, we don't want to rip out all the hull caulking unless we're talking about a real, bona fide caulk job—which might want to be done as a project in itself, say, before a long cruise or before putting the boat up for sale. Again, the books were somewhat vague, saying at one point that this is a developed skill, but one that requires little brain cell activity. I didn't get too far into the process, because as far as I could tell, not a lot of cotton needed to be driven. The books were a little cautionary when talking about twisting and driving cotton into big, fat openings that suddenly petered out into slim little cracks better handled by the old goop from the tube. So I caulked with cotton where it was wide and deep and covered the cotton with a line of tearful Ted's good old white goop.

Things at the marina were still pretty quiet. I soon found out why. Chip and his buddies had decided not return to St. Paul after all and to stay in Florida. This seemed to spread a sense of relief around the docks, though no one spoke about it directly; the spring work days were relaxed and peaceful.

Three weekends of hull work found me sanding the topsides and applying that special black gold hull paint all around. My Rustoleum experiment, while successful, just wasn't fun any more. Besides, I had put my deposit on a slip at a real sailboat yacht marina and felt a growing sense of obligation to give this project the best of my efforts.

A last-minute flurry of interior work got me into the space for the new head, and I managed to install the sink and sink counter, as well as some oak paneling along the inside port bulkhead. The handsome new pot was stored up forward under the sleeping platform, which I'll now start calling the forecastle (pronounced foc's'le if you're into sailor talk). I took a four-day vacation dovetailed with Memorial Day weekend and spent the last day before the big move stopping up all the holes and inlets and outlets anywhere on the boat that might let water in when we launched. I also asked the new guys at Watchamajig marina to drag my mast out of the storage barn. I needed to revarnish it and make sure it was still in okay shape after almost two years on the flat. That was, as usual, a request far too complicated for quick action. When the following Saturday arrived and Georgia and I got to the yard to work on the mast, we were not surprised to find it was still in the barn behind tons of boat stuff. Three days before the truck arrived, the mast finally appeared. We frantically sanded and varnished—three times.

On the morning of the 27th, I was really wired. A million things to do and no control over any of it. RJ, the nice young kid from Shorewood Marina, had come over with an electrician, and they installed a new antenna and anchor light at the masthead, wired in a new steaming light about halfway down the mast, and hooked up all the standing rigging. The rigging had been coiled up under my coffee table at home; now it was neatly bound to the mast for travel. The whole rig, lying beside the long driveway in the St. Paul marina, looked like a Wellsian space probe. The sun was bright and the day was fresh as could be; perfect for this exciting move out of the river bottoms and onto the big lake. I still couldn't believe the luck and the timing of this whole arrangement.

*   *   *

A big, blue semi truck with a special lowboy trailer showed up right on time. Of course, true to form, the old Travelift at Watchamajig was out of sync, so the boys couldn't keep it running. It finally got LILIBET up off the cradle and around to the truck bed, where the lift's engine coughed and wheezed and quit, leaving the boat hanging in the air over the truck. Everyone was in a state, and I could easily tell they would be glad to see this big old sailboat disappear over the horizon. They sent out for new spark plugs. Meanwhile the truck driver built a cradle for the hull, and we all pretended not to worry. Finally, after ten or twelve starts and stops, the lift deposited LILIBET onto the truck bed with a final downward chug that made my heart do a back flip. Everyone heaved a sigh of relief, and in spite of the Peter Principle we did get going on time. I followed the truck and my boat up the long hill out of the river bottoms and into the rest of the world. No one waved good bye.

It was very strange to see that boat cruising along the freeway in four lanes of traffic with little visible means of support. Within the hour she was breezing along country roads past the trees by the big lake, and then we were at the new marina.

Actually the marina is not new but rather an old-fashioned place. It's like what you might remember from your childhood at a lake in the northern part of the Midwest, even though it was in one of the toniest sections of the Twin Cities. I was ever so pleased to have found this bit of 1950s rusticity still in place.

There's a dredging company right next door, with cranes

and piles of rocks and wooden poles like telephone poles, which they use for sea walls and docks. It is probably the only industrial business operating on the lake, and it probably does so because of its importance to the lake shore (it barges pilings and boulders for seawall rebuilding all around the lake). I'll bet it has some kind of grandfather agreement with the town of Shorewood to remain in business.

There's a driveway leading in from the road past the dredging company and back to the yacht club, which sits in a protected bay of the lake. The clubhouse is a really well-kept old rambling house, low slung with a series of add-ons with offices, bathrooms, a wonderfully quaint knotty-pine clubroom with a kitchen and fireplace, and a newly added workshop. The clubroom is hung with old yacht regalia—ropes, steering wheels, blocks and tackle, pictures of the members, and various racing trophies stashed on shelves. It's cozy. On the water side, overlooking the docks, a series of large weather-worn decks wrap around about half of the clubhouse. The decks look over a nice tree-shaded lawn that leads down to the docks.

When I pulled into the yacht yard, the Rocket Crane crew was already setting up. It looked like a missile launch. Their truck and rig were new and painted red and white. Big outriggers extended from the truck bed under the crane. It was a beehive of activity. There was a reporter from the local paper, the boatyard crew, our daughter Jordan and her friends, the truck hauler, who stayed to help get the boat in the water, and the Rocket guys in their red hard hats.

I checked the scene and searched out John, the owner of the marina. It appeared he was hiding out in one of the upstairs rooms, peeking out through the blinds at the scene. Actually, he was nervous, but not because of the launch activity per se. I found out later that a long standing tiff between John and the guy who owns the dredging company—a curmudgeon out of the same mold—was the real issue. The origin of the argument seems to have blurred into the mists of time, but these old gentlemen seemed to enjoy any opportunity to fuel the embers. The giant crane accompanied by the boat hauler's truck, which was parked temporarily on the dredging company property while the hauler waited for the crane to be set up, made John itchy, so he was really avoiding the inevitable theatrical tongue lashing of his neighbor.

I gave Jordan the photo documentation assignment, and while the guys in hard hats fitted slings to LILIBET's hull, I grabbed a ladder and went on board to let go the truck straps and prep the 110-volt sump pump for duty. By the time I got down Rocket was ready to lift her off. Wow.

The lift off was a thrill, because that giant crane had such a fine ability to just ease the weight off the truck until the boat was hanging in the air. They let it hang while everyone took a moment to check for problems and to see if she were still level. The crane operator looked my way for the signal, which was given with a nod, and up she went in the air. Nice and smooth. One of the guys guided her around like a big gas balloon in a parade. They got her over the water and slowly slid her down.

LILIBET hangs in the crane slings at the Shorewood Yacht Club on her way to the launch where the water is comfortably deep, Spring 2004

I must say that this launching was much less stressful than the river launch down that long ramp. Everyone of the dozen or so people involved, most of whom had never met, joined together to make sure the old girl was properly welcomed to her new home. When LILIBET was clearly floating in the water, I signaled the crane operator and asked if I could go onboard. He gave the okay, and I dropped down into the saloon and plugged the sump pump into the shore power. Water was flooding in like last year, but I was not panicky. It felt great to trust the wood to swell. There was one small leak up forward. I could hear water trickling in and tried to visualize where I had forgotten to caulk. Peter, Jordan's friend who works the fishing boats in Alaska during the summer, dug down in the forward bilge and located the leak. I tucked in some cotton caulking by feel, and it slowed down. Other than that, there was some small seeping that filled the bottom of the boat with water, which the pump handled nicely.

Despite the need to keep an eye on the water level for the rest of the day, things went forward very smoothly. In a couple of hours the leaking was stopped. By now John, the marina owner, was on board checking things out, lifting a rope here, examining some brightwork there; he seemed pleased with his decision to allow the boat in his marina. I sure was.

Back on shore the guys were getting ready to raise the mast—for me a historical event. The mast at 55 feet was very long and quite limber. As we dragged it around on dollies back in St. Paul, it flexed and moved like a noodle. Now it had at least a couple hundred pounds of metal rigging hung on it, and I was really nervous about lifting it up and sliding it through the cabin roof down into the maststep. Apparently so was everyone else, because a long discussion took place. The marina guys had one version of how it should be done, and the crane guys had another. "But if we lift it here it could do this" and "Yeah, but if we lift it here it might do that." It was a good case of folks trying to do the best thing. But the day was wearing on, so when finally they all looked at me, and then I said, "Okay, let's let these crane guys do their work," everyone looked relieved.

A big nylon sling was fastened to the mast just below the bottom spreaders, which were about two-thirds of the way up the mast. The lift began, and the mast slowly stood

Captain Jack (on the right) hold his breath while yardman R.J. and
the crane ease the mast from horizontal to vertical

straight up as it left the ground and headed in the air over
to the boat. As the heel lined up with the hole, guided by a
couple of good hands, RJ and I went below to steer it down
and into the maststep on the keel. The accuracy and finesse
of that crane driver was superb. The maststep itself was just
a simple "step" slot, or mortise, in which the heel of the spar
was seated. It was held temporarily in place by its own
weight and the metal collar, or partner, in the cabin roof
while the rigging was set up. In all my midnight imaginings
I could never have predicted how easy this process seemed
to be. And it continued that way through the rest of the day.

Rocket packed up its machinery while the yard guys set
up the rigging. As a guide, RJ used my old photos taken in
Maryland of the mast, forestay, backstay, shrouds, running

backstays, and all the rest. Every so often he'd call me over to get my opinion on what went where. I didn't know, of course, but when the day was done, there she sat, the water-line at the boottop where it belonged, that nice, tall wooden mast standing straight, with all its wire running to the right places. It was an event and a half.

Finally everyone was gone, and it was me and the boat on a sunny May evening. I called Georgia to report in, and then stayed on board all night watching the water rise and fall in the bilge while the seams slowly swelled shut. At 4 a.m. I went to sleep in the new forecastle bunk. I was up at 8 a.m. that morning, a little stiff and groggy, and I met the yard guys, who cranked up their mini marina towboat and hauled LILIBET around to her position on the dock. What a treat.

The following week I actually located a diesel engine repair and maintenance company that agreed to come out and put the Perkins into shape, but things were moving a little too fast. I decided to hold off on engine work until my checkbook stopped smoking. And a good thing it was too, because later I went with a local guy.

I took a deep breath and asked myself the wonderful question: what's left? Or better said, what are the big things left to do? I had a very lengthy to-do list, now dog-eared and covered with scribbles and a multitude of rewrites. First, finish the overhead in the forecastle and the overhead above the sink and stove on the port side of the main saloon. This would entail ripping down some old headliner (not original stuff) and soaking the overhead planking (the

She stands! With the rigging streaming down, the 55-foot mast is finally in position to rejoin the boat

underside of the deck) with rot poison of some kind to be sure it got its little preventive jigger of rum before the cover went on, and brushing on a protective layer of Gorilla glue—my own self-indulgent treatment—to give the underside of the deck a good coating of an indestructible chemical. Then applying a surface of birch veneer screwed to the cross beams, and finally trimming and painting to a finished condition. About three good work sessions, I thought.

Next came work on the head. Build the floor and support for the new toilet, build the surrounding bulkhead, build a door, hook up the facilities—I guess it would be mostly head work for awhile. Then there would be the engine work, and the wiring to get us legal for night cruising, and the state of Minnesota registration thing . . . Hmm, I think there could be some tax due on my original purchase . . . I promised we would sail before October.

Speaking of engine work, in the interim between launch and actually scheduling a mechanic for the Perkins, I determined to learn as much about marine diesel engines as I could. I even had a notion that I might learn enough by reading and a little applied knowledge that at some future time I would be good at. As has always been the ticket, I stationed two books strategically—one, an engine shop manual for the Perkins, on my boat and another, a general diesel do-it-yourself book, right next to the seat of ease in our home bathroom. In the past, this worked well. By simply spending brief periods of time reading bits chosen randomly throughout the literature, one can become darned conversant in nearly any subject—boatbuilding, sailing, wood maintenance, varnishes, paint—all that stuff. There seems to be an imprinting process with written words that eventually gives one a fairly complete view of the subject and a certain retention when viewed from this location. Interestingly, this same imprinting never seems to work quite so well when sitting on a regular chair—no matter what kind: rocking, strata-lounger, club chair, whatever. So I thought I would employ that same old tried-and-true method and get cozy with my diesel engine.

After three or four weeks however, it became clear that the miracle wasn't happening. Mostly what I read was how much can go wrong with what I've always believed to be a nearly indestructible engine. As my library hours increased, so did my apprehension. Hundreds of things can go wrong, it seems, and since everything is connected together, it's like a domino effect, all bad news. Fluids that don't flow, air-locked passageways, white smoke vs. blue smoke vs. black smoke—all indicating something terrible, such as a cracked head, water in the fuel, water in the crankcase, blockage in the water intake, valves that don't seat correctly, piston rings gone south. And that's just for beginners. To make matters worse, five minutes after I read about all this stuff, it's gone from my mind except for a lingering residue of anxiety. And then there's the imagined bad treatment the engine may or may not have received before I got the boat or, heaven forbid, what about over in Saint Paul? When I shut her down last summer after my little in-and-out spree at the St. Paul dock, was the engine overheated? Like, yeah—there was a ton of blue smoke then! What if I blew out a gizmo or something? What if the guys at the yard didn't really truly drain all the water—every last drop—out of the engine before winter? Who knows? I began yakking it up around the new marina.

Soon it was pretty general knowledge that I needed a mechanic. Finally, I met the guy who works on boats at Shorewood and spent an hour going over the Perkins with him. His real job was engine mechanic on jet airliners out at the airport—Northwest headquarters. He liked to run a side business fixing boat engines and doing wiring jobs. I was thinking this might be overkill but hey, if he kept the air busses flying, I bet he could get a little four-banger diesel back in shape. He looked things over, made the right moves, made intelligent and limited conversation, took a few notes, paged through my Perkins shop manual. His name was Jim, and he contracted work through the marina, so he was in the neighborhood. Okay, this could work.

Sailing Lilibet

By July 4th it was evident that LILIBET's two-year restoration project was just about as complete as it would get for now. Georgia and I were really getting the "go to sea" bug. My job list was more than half done. The head was now the only big unfinished deal, and since we were only going to take short cruises this year—engine work allowing—I was in the mood to coast on it, at least for a bit, especially since we were now actually able to spend time on the boat without feeling like we were camping out. This July 4th would be in fact our first overnight on board LILIBET.

The weather was better than perfect. For July in Minnesota, which is usually hot and sticky, this was surely better than most. Just a nice, sunny, warm, clear day. And only one of many, it turned out, because the whole summer seemed to stay delightful, meaning low humidity and moderate temperatures. When fall arrived, there was lots of talk in the marina about what a bad summer it had been. Too much rain and cool temperatures for decent sailing. Wow, I thought, these guys haven't been to Seattle.

We puttered around the decks all day after a morning

drive out from the city and joined the marina crowd at the club for a Fourth of July picnic. Being on the end slip was really wonderful. There's a little island out about three hundred yards from the dock, with channels on either side where the sailboats come and go. The lake breeze comes in from there, too and as the night comes on, there's a feeling of supreme peacefulness as the boat moves under you.

Fireworks were towed out into the lake on a barge from the dredging company docks next door and went around the point to Excelsior Bay, where they blasted prettily into the darkened sky. We sacked out on the new cushions Georgia made for the forecastle bed. We left the cockpit hatches open, as well as the forward cabin hatch, which is right above the bed. I remember lying there in the dark boat listening to the sounds as it moved gently in the faint breeze. And I remember how restful it was to feel just the breath of night air come down the hatch overhead and pass aft toward the open cockpit. It felt a little as if the boat were breathing.

Minnesota rainstorms can come roaring across the prairie rather suddenly in summer. Some time around 4 a.m. I felt a shot of cool wind rush through the cabin and could hear a heightened gnashing of the dock lines as LILIBET surged around like a pony tied in its stall. If one thought boats really had a life, it would be a sure bet that she was kicking up her heels, because this was the closest thing to dirty weather in the water since her sea days. There was also plenty of halyard banging going on with all the boats around us as the wind picked up. A couple of big, cold raindrops fell like pebbles through the hatch and onto my bare stomach. I knew it was just the beginning of one of our summer soakers.

As we gathered our sleepy wits to close the ports and hatches, a brilliant flash of lightning filled the night and a blast of thunder vibrated through the deck and down the hull. Georgia's wonderful rain cover lay rolled up at the forward end of the doghouse, and we came out of the cabin into a drenching downpour. Lightning slashed across the lake and lit up the marina and the water around us in a steady and really dramatic display—each flash accompanied by a clap of thunder that seemed to originate in the wet air right next to the boat. We each took a side, port and starboard, and unrolling the big cover as we went forward, stretched and clipped it to its matching stanchions. Every lightning flash lit up the deck and rigging like a halide light show as we worked our way back over the doghouse and cockpit. Finally, the cover was secure and the rain drummed on it like a parade of soldiers marching off to war.

We toweled off and checked the interior for leaks. I wasn't surprised to find a couple forward of the mast; one seemed to originate under a cabin light (that's not a lamp, but a bracketed lens that lets daylight into the dark cabin). A screw had probably lost its bedding compound. This aggravating leak, however, showed up right over the sleeping space, and I spent the remaining hours till daylight snoozing with a wet towel wadded up next to me to catch the drips. We awoke mid-morning to a wonderfully clear, sunny day, the world all washed clean and bright, including our boat.

This was the first of many such weekends spent overnight at the marina. Georgia and I would pack our boat

clothes into one of the original "BeeBags," those old yellow-
and-black-striped overnight bags Georgia had made for our
trips into Seattle from Vashon Island, to spend weekends on
the BIG DIPPER. Talk about old memories. Nowadays, we'd
take a novel or two and stop at Ricky's Market along the way
for munchies, then enjoy the drive through the countryside
to the docks.

Belonging to this yacht club thing was something new
to us. Membership came with the moorage, so you didn't
have to pass any tests or have your pedigree checked. Instead, you started getting invited to the nearly weekly social
gatherings that happened most Friday or Saturday nights.
Don't forget, with a water season only six months long,
Minnesota boaters must cram lots of activity into the summer. At first, Georgia feared the critical eyes of the club
members who might find fault with our old wooden lady in
this batch of spiffy fiberglass. As I said, we'd been turned
down on a slot at the dock only a year before.

Truth be told, however, the Tupperware fleet at
Shorewood wasn't totally perfect, and LILIBET looked like a
class act out there at the end of the dock. That black hull
and mega brightwork just flashed in the sun. She was a
wonder, both for her good lines and age plus the amount of
obvious work that went into bringing her up to condition.
We got lots of compliments. I had a delightful moment one
afternoon as I walked down the dock and came to a large
fellow sanding the teak platform under his bow pulpit. He
grinned sheepishly when I complimented his work, and we

LILIBET tied in her new slip at the end of the dock, Shorewood Yacht Club, Summer 2004

both laughed when I mentioned how terrific it made me feel to see someone else working on wood.

The club membership was all over the demographic map. Some young, some old, some wealthy, some not. It was an easy mix to be with. No ascots and very few white deck pants. Lots of soft middles and a fair amount of overhang, which put the old sailor stereotype image at bay. They were a welcoming, cordial crowd, and I was not as intimidated as I thought I'd be. Most people were very friendly and not very competitive, although there was a group of racing cronies who slammed out on the lake early, and shouted back and forth at each other in the most yachty possible way. Georgia and I would show up on Saturday morning in jeans and T-shirts, scrub a little wood, lay on some varnish, take a snooze on the new mattress pads in the forecastle or on the cockpit benches, listen to the radio, and watch the sun move toward the evening horizon. The lake was full of fish and turtles, and they came by for visits. Along about dark, we would take the truck into the quaint little lake town called Excelsior and have a pizza. Later, back on board, we would read and fall asleep. It was like being in a totally different state—I'm not sure where—and by the time we loaded up for the thirty-minute drive into Minneapolis on Sunday, we were rested but tired, sunburned and peaceful, glad we had found this old wooden sailboat.

August 2004 at home, and the big old mainsail was spread out on the living room floor. It had seen a lot of ocean and needed repairs. With the reality of actually sailing coming over the horizon, it was past time to tend to the stitching on this monster. With Georgia's fleet of industrial sewing machines in the spare bedroom, it was fast work to re-sew the large flap of loose cloth along the leech (the trailing edge of the sail). It had come loose in a storm and revealed a light rope-edge support. The tougher part, however, was re-stitching the foot (the bottom edge of the sail) and the luff (the leading edge, which goes right up against the mast). These edges are sewn around a piece of half-inch rope that holds the sail slides—flat bronze hardware that fit into a groove on the mast and on the boom. This sounds more complicated than it is.

The sailcloth is like iron, so a regular needle won't pass through it, and you can't run all this stuff through a sewing machine. The answer is a small hand-stitching device with an awl-like needle, waxed-nylon thread, and a wooden handle. You push the needle through the tough fabric, make a loop in the thread as you pull the needle back, and run a needle attached to the other end of the thread through the loop to form a running stitch as you go. Some people get very good at this. Georgia after a few practices mastered the process quite well. I, on the other hand, probably won't get that good. In fact, in my last try, I did only about a foot in an hour. My guess, though, is that if I were becalmed out at sea and had some sail work to do in the days and weeks of waiting for a wind, I might do a good deal better.

August in Minnesota can be a tough month. Especially when you've got something of an unfinished boat project. In this part of the country we can tell winter is on its way even in August. Things change. The light, the color of the sky, the random rain and wind and cooling temperatures flirting with a few of those hot, sticky days. Many of the suburban sailors have lost their edge. The docks are less populated, and more of the guys show up by themselves to run her out for an hour after work, then drive off to dinner at home. We still dress in our Hawaiian party shirts and khaki shorts, but ya know, we're thinking sweatshirts. And, we're thinking "haulout."

October 15 is the official time to be out of the water, but things start happening around the first of the month, so in August, you start counting the days of boating that remain in the season. I had the blues, because it had been too long since I met up with the air bus mechanic and because there had been too little action in the engine department. It was starting to get embarrassing when people asked me if I had the boat out over the weekend. Some were asking if we would get it out at all this year. So there were plenty of dark thoughts running through my head as I drove out to the marina on August 7 for my usual check in on progress.

Rounding the corner of the dock and heading for the familiar grab on the shrouds for a hoist aboard, I was surprised and pleased to see the rain cover unhooked and movement in the cockpit. "He's here!" I thought. I surprised Jim the mechanic; he jumped a little when he saw me, but he looked hopeful—probably reflecting my own expression. "I got her running," he said. "Purrs like a kitten."

Being elated, I found it hard to contain myself, so I just asked for any bad news found along the way. To my relief, there was very little, and certainly nothing big. The leaking injector had been rebuilt and now stood proudly in line with its three brothers. The fuel and oil filters had been changed. The big battery had been hooked up at long last. Most of the new gauges now worked, with the exception of the oil-pressure gauge, which needed a sending unit, and the tachometer, which may never work—it seems to be something not meant for this engine.

Some wiring was left, mostly the alternator, which charges the batteries when the engine is running, and the battery separator switch. I asked if we could run it, and he reached over to the starboard mahogany panel I had installed a year earlier and turned the key. Instantly the little Perkins rumbled to life. No smoke, and the engine growled along smoothly. I couldn't think of what to say, so I just yelled "This is huge!" over the noise. He agreed. I was ready to take her out on the lake that same day, but without the alternator I decided to wait. Dead batteries are a real drag when you're not a competent sailor. He said he'd be back on Monday to finish up, but of course that didn't happen. I stopped by on my way home from work and couldn't help but start her up again. Great!

For the next three weeks we hung on breathlessly waiting for the elusive airplane mechanic to hook the three wires from the alternator to whatever was necessary. It seemed so simple, and I'm here to tell you it is simple once you see it done. Any half-baked car enthusiast who reads this will undoubtedly call me a nerd, but in the meantime anyone around the docks who poked their nose into the Perkins pit on LILIBET just shook their head. Like everything else on my boat, there is a little too much history in the engine compartment for the average Joe. By the third week we were starting to get offers of rides on our neighbor's boats. Well meant of course, but!

On the next Saturday, I checked in with the yard shop to see if anyone knew about Jim the mechanic's schedule. To my chagrin, I was told he had gone up north for a week's stay at his cabin. Obligated as I felt to continue working with this guy, and not wanting to piss off the boys at this sweet new marina, I made up my mind to find someone—anyone with a pair of pliers and some grease under his nails—to get this thing going. Next day I made my way through the phone book and finally found a mobile engine repair outfit that would travel out to the docks. We set a time for the following Monday, and I held my breath. Monday morning I took off work, got to the docks early, and opened her up. When the agreed meeting time passed by, I called the number scribbled on an old yellow sticky note crumpled up in my pocket. The guy on the other end had forgotten. By now, of course, I was getting used to what perhaps is a universal Murphy's Law in the world of boats—don't depend on boat guys. He apologized and promised to meet me any time I wished. "How about five o'clock tonight?" I said. I could hear the reluctance in the millisecond pause, but he promised to be there. And so he was.

The job took about an hour and several phone calls for consultation with his partner, who was probably sitting at home having a brewski or two, but after two or three false starts, we could see the meters registering charge when the engine was running. I was stuck with the assignment of finding an idiot light to hook between the ignition switch and the exciter wire, which I did the next day, but guess what—the long road to diesel power credibility was won. Yeah, it's just a simple operation, but what a big deal. Turn on the key, watch the amber idiot light go on, switch the engine on, listen with pride as it chugs to life and rumbles away, then cast your eye on the voltmeter and see it reaching to the positive horizon. Climb the companionway steps through the open hatchway to the cockpit, rev her up a bit, untie the lines, drop her into reverse, and ease on out of the slip. And that's exactly what we did the following weekend.

LIFT OFF

Like everything else in this little restoration adventure, setting LILIBET free from the dock was not an immediate or instant production. First you have to figure in all the built-up jitters and excitement of her former stinkpot captain and his mate after reading two-years' worth of adventures on the high seas before bedtime. Waves as tall as a ten-story building, masts blown away, boats turning cartwheels in the water and landing sideways on some rocky coast. It's ridiculous really, knowing that the waters of Lake Minnetonka have little relationship to the big seas this boat had weathered. Yet there we were, not quite ready to actually get our now almost finished project out on the lake.

Honestly, there were two reasons. One had some small reality, the other didn't, and they both caused a flurry of delays. First of all, I was slightly crewless. That's crewless, not clueless, although somewhere I'm sure there's an argument about that. I needed to have some salty dogs on deck for the first bit. Georgia agreed. I agreed, but we were new to this place, this cozy little old-fashioned lake club.

There are dogs and then there are salty dogs, and I was hesitant to find myself in a windy situation with a bunch of good intentions and a boatload of well-meaning experts, when I just barely knew an outhaul from a topping lift—so I waited a little.

The other point was that a big part of my own personal hesitation came from the host of well meant, but slightly sour, comments over time from family and friends about the nerve it must take to believe that someone as elderly (inferred) and inexperienced in sailing as I was would actually attempt such a thing.

Remember, this is a part of the world where people believe that changing addresses more than twice in a lifetime is pretty risky business, still it doesn't stop them from directing traffic whenever they can. My response has always been, "Well hey, ya know." Pretty benign, and it never got me into any fist fights, so that's good. But things now seemed far from the old days when there were always a bunch of good-timers willing to share a day's adventure and a couple of beers—risks be damned. I'll admit, grudgingly, that age does factor in, so now there I was standing on the dock feeling a little unsure.

Georgia and I tinkered with our rigging, laid down another coat of varnish here and there, and suggested to each other that we just fire up the engine and go learn to sail. One of our neighbors, sensing our dilemma, kindly invited us aboard his boat for a Sunday sail on a day of light wind. We accepted gladly, and climbed aboard while he and his wife let go the dock lines and backed out into the lake.

Gene and Norma are good lake sailors and comfortable to be with. I took the tiller while Gene guided me through the flack fields of water hazard markers that dot the exit from our moorage. As we shut off the engine and raised the sails, a little wind stirred the telltales on the mainsail, and we heeled slightly as the boat got under way. We talked about wind direction and speed, tacking and jibing, a little line handling. Other boats from our marina slid by, and we all waved. I could feel the boat respond to the breeze and tried to get a handle on this sailing thing. After about an hour we headed back. Just as we entered the marina, Gene asked if we all were now taking LILIBET out for a spin. What a great way to get us going. And what a kindly thing to do.

Georgia and I gave a hand in docking their boat and then hustled over to LILIBET in a kind of breathless Wow-ism to make ready. I cranked up Mr. Perkins, and he rumbled obediently to life. No smoke. Remembering the embarrassing in and out exercise last summer at the St. Paul marina, I was a little tense, but I put my mind back a decade-plus when I used to run the BIG DIPPER and DENALI in and out of some pretty complicated moorages. Go for it, Jack!

Gene and Norma showed up with Duncan, another sailor and former commodore of the yacht club. Also a very nice person. They helped Georgia untie the forward lines and I got the after ones. Suddenly we were floating free. I put the rudder straight, and when everyone was aboard, dropped Mr. Perkins into reverse and slid smoothly out of the slip. I was thrilled at the solid feel of her underfoot and the quick response when I shifted to forward. We made a nice, tidy circle in front of the docks and glided toward the red-and-green channel markers guarding the narrow outlet to the big lake. I steeled myself for the keel dragging I expected, but felt none as we eased our way into open water.

I neglected to say that the old depthfinder was not working, as I didn't have time to get it fixed before the move from St. Paul. So here we were out in the lake, guessing where our bottom was. I think everyone else had the same concern. I stayed in the middle of the channel and motored out into the big lake. What a thrill to be on this boat, free from the dock. Sailing or not, she just felt great moving through the water. The sun shone bright on the deck, reflecting all that varnished oak; the teak decks glistened. It was also a thrill to see people moving about the decks in anticipation of raising the sails.

Several weeks earlier, Georgia and I had secured the mainsail on the boom, carefully inserting the big old slides into the bronze groove that runs the length of the boom. Georgia had made beautiful sail covers of the same dark maroon fabric as the sun shade and the sail bags, so we were right jolly color-coordinated. The staysail was secured in place forward of the mast, though it wasn't rigged correctly, as I found out a couple of weeks later. For now, however, everything was hunky-dory.

The breeze was feeble—and that's a good thing for beginner sailors. At least for these beginner sailors. The lads, as I will now call any crew, man or woman, kind enough to accompany us at sea, were wonderfully nice. Duncan, who made it his job to handle the rigging, stood close to the gear for the boom topping lift and suggested we head up into the wind and raise the sail. That was easy, and once we were pointed directly into the breeze I suggested that we should raise the boom by means of the topping lift to get it off the gallows, or boom crutch—a kind of rack just aft of the cockpit that supports the boom when it is not in use. Duncan, who I'm sure knows as much as most do about rigging, asked in a very polite way, "And where would that topping lift be (pray tell)?"

"Well," I answered, "I believe it's right there to your left. That white line with the two blocks attached."

"Oh, of course," he answered back. He untied the knot that held the lift line and gingerly hoisted the boom off the gallows so that it swung easily free. And so it went.

The mainsail was raised using the old and outrageously heavy cast-bronze winch handle. About two thirds of the way up the mast the slides began to hang up on years' worth of corrosion in the track, so it was a tussle. Georgia stood by guiding the sail upward from its big wad of folded fabric, and Duncan cranked mightily on the ancient winch. After several up-down, up-down attempts to free the slides, the sail finally reached the top of the mast and stood proudly slack in the afternoon sun. Duncan smiled broadly under his sweaty brow as we turned sideways to the breeze. I gave Gene the wheel and dashed below to shut down the engine.

As I said, there really was no breeze to speak of, so we just moved along with the sail occasionally puffing out enough to see the water go past us. Gene talked about reading the wind by the telltales, the riffles on the water, and the pointer mounted on the head of my mast. He also recommended that I buy a handheld wind-direction indicator from an electronics shop. We talked about the lake and the boat, and someone came motoring by in their own sailboat and snapped some pictures. Finally, it was obvious we weren't having a ride, so we dropped the mainsail—not without a struggle—and I cranked up Mr. Perkins again. As we eased into the channel going home Gene said, "Well, only one more challenge."

"Right," I answered. "Getting her into the slip." We all laughed, but I was a little nervous. By now I had a feel for LILIBET's movement and how she responded to gear shifts and engine control. It made things a lot better. With no wind, the task was easy. I made the turn into the slip, cut the engine speed, shifted into reverse, revved Mr. Perkins just a little—till I could see our forward motion almost stop—dropped her into neutral, and coasted in. It was simply perfect until I lost my concentration and didn't shut off the engine. Somehow I thought the boat was moving when it wasn't, so everyone had a moment of "grab on" while I got it together. No damage was done, and we ended the day with lots of thank-yous and we'll-do-it-agains.

The next weekend Georgia and I greased up the slide track on the mast and raised the mainsail to lubricate the groove all the way up. It worked. Then we decided to go it alone. At least do a little putt out on the lake. Maybe not actually raise the sails, but just get some boat handling in. We discussed our moves, mostly the return to the dock and how we'd manage the tie-up. Georgia retied all the dock lines so they weren't so complicated. I started the engine, let it

Georgia relaxing in the cockpit after a day of brightwork "maintenance varnishing"

warm up, checked the bilge for anything unusual, and un-plugged the shore power cord. Then we slipped off the lines, backed out, and made our turn out through the channel markers.

It was super being just the two of us on our great old yacht. It was also very *déjà vu*. Looking aft at Georgia han-dling the big silver wheel seemed so natural and so very much like the million times we had done this in Seattle. Well, of course we had—this was just a different boat. Both of us remarked about the solid, steady way she plowed through the water and how quickly she responded to the wheel. Nice, but we really should learn this sailing thing.

We cruised out into the big part of the lake, where the breeze was strong enough for a little sailing, but we decided we were not confident enough to handle the sails alone yet, so we made a couple of circles and headed for home port. All in all it was a good cruise for our first time alone. I listened to the engine and watched the gauges to see if all was well. It seemed it was. Coming back in was as good as before, and we were pleased when a group of neighbors partying on a boat a few slots down jumped to our assistance and were surprised by how well we managed to ease LILIBET into place.

I took some time off from work the following week, early September, thinking I would spend every day on the water. It didn't turn out that way. Some good intentions about coming out to help sail by my dock mates fell short. I probably wasn't welcoming enough, or perhaps the thought of getting involved in some old wooden boat disaster at sea might have caused a little pause.

On Sunday evening I called Frank, an old pal of ours who had done plenty of sailing, including some ocean sailing, and is one of those people from the past who used to like adventure and a couple of beers just to have fun. Those were, of course, during our hippie days, but it turns out he still did enjoy a little thrill—with only slight reservations in that now he, like me, is entering his late years and has a successful married life, a good business, and plenty of relaxed Minnesota sundowns to look forward to. We both checked the weather channel that night; it said the wind would be twenty five to thirty miles per hour all day. I don't know what that amounts to in knots—nautical miles per hour—but it seemed pretty windy. In fact it was very windy. Unfortunately, Georgia had to go to her work, so half the team would be missing. If I knew how much fun this was going to be, I would have insisted she take a sick day and come along.

On Monday morning Frank called and said, "Hey, let's go sailing." He said he'd pick me up in a half hour and we'd ride in his vintage Jaguar. This was Frank's special car, big and black, with tan leather seats, and which he only took on special drives, never in the winter. I knew this was going to be fun.

Frank is a gentleman artist, gallery owner, and sort of real estate procurement officer for his friends and relatives. He and I have known each other for many years, and we have crossed paths in far-off, out-of-the-way places over the course of those years. For a guy who lives much of his life on a little farm in Clayton, Wisconsin, he is quite a world traveler and has sailed on the ocean from various ports, including New Zealand. Because of their deep roots in Minnesota, however, Frank and his wife know just about everyone who is anyone who does things in the Twin Cities. As I eased into the Jag, he suggested we call his friend George the goldsmith, who was also a good sailor and with whom Frank had sailed a lot. I had met George several times at various parties; it sounded good to me. Actually, it was great.

We drove through Minneapolis on our way to George's and talked boats. Frank had always enjoyed our boating adventures and, given a less connected life in Minnesota, might have found a big old hull for himself. We also both have a long record of hatching up unusual lifestyle choices built around art. It's reassuring to have friends of the same mindset.

George was waiting in his driveway; he got into the back seat, and we headed for the western suburbs and Lake Minnetonka. Frank had seen the boat but George had not, and he was very complimentary. They pitched right in to help remove the weather cover and tie down any loose gear on deck. It was evident both were familiar with boats. Soon we had LILIBET ready to go. I was nervous as a cat, but they seemed quite at ease.

It was a beautiful late summer day, and the sun was warm on our shoulders. I could see the wind in the trees and was excited to go sailing for real. Once we cleared the channel and got into open water, I gave Frank the helm and went forward to help George raise the topping lift and then the mainsail. The boat was headed up into the wind. It took George and me a minute to be sure all the lines were right and the winch worked just so, and I could tell right away that George was both thorough and knowledgeable. I had remembered to bring along the two flat oak sail battens to put into the sail before we raised it, but of course didn't do it in the rush of things, so George dropped the sail back down and Frank held the battens for me to grab as the pockets came into reach. By now the shifty winds had shifted, and while Frank kept her as dead into the wind as he could I inserted the battens and George cranked the sail back up.

It was pretty dramatic. The wind, huffing away at perhaps 20 miles per hour, made the big maroon sail flap wildly as it went up. Suddenly one of the battens—a thin piece of wood about 4 inches wide and 30 inches long—just shook itself out of its pocket and went sailing off into the water about 60 yards away. The lads were plenty ready to drop the sail and go rescue the stick, but I wasn't going to let a fly-away batten stop us now, so I said no and we secured the mainsail. Frank turned the boat away from the wind and the sail filled with a wonderful thump. LILIBET immediately heeled over, and we were on our way. After the initial thrill register going over the top on the wowser gauge, I dropped into the cabin and shut down the engine. I came back up and gingerly made my way along the high side of the boat to help George raise the staysail.

Weeks earlier, Georgia and I had debated how to rig the staysail. In the old photos, I could see a single sheet hooked to the tack (in sailor talk, a sheet is a sail-trimming line and the tack is the aft bottom corner on a headsail). We could never figure out how one did any kind of sail trimming, because the line leading back to the cockpit would always be hung up on one side of the mast, so that seemed strange. After due deliberation, I clipped on a double-sheet rig, so there was a sheet running from the tack back to the cockpit on each side of the mast, allowing for trimming from both sides of the mast. Right or wrong, that's how it was today, and neither George nor Frank had any better solutions.

Another rigging decision Georgia and I had made, and which turned out to be totally wrong, was to rig what looked like a small topping lift that hung from the forward side of the mast just below the first set of spreaders. At least it looked like a topping lift at the time. As of this writing, I still don't know what that was for, but it sure wasn't for the staysail. It's on my list of "what the hell is that for?" items that I hope to figure out as I get better at this.

I know this sounds wonderfully unsailorish, and totally incomprehensible, but isn't it fun?

The staysail on this cutter rig has a little wooden boom that is fastened at the forward end to the deck by an articulating cleat; this allows the sail to be set on one side of the centerline or the other as the wind requires. The boom looks club-like, so the whole setup is called a clubfooted staysail. I do believe it's called a staysail, because it helps steady the boat. In my zeal to get everything running smoothly, I decided the after end of the boom needed something to raise it up so that when it swung wide in a crisp wind it would clear the shrouds (shrouds are wire stays that support the mast from side to side and keep the mast from falling down).

Here now, conveniently, was this nice little line with a block on it just where I needed it to hitch up the staysail boom. Cool. On this fine day, we watched as that very staysail bellied out in perfect harmony with the mainsail. But I had most definitely rigged it wrong, for in very short order the screws holding the stainless-steel U-bolt that held my little topping lift to the mast just below the spreaders pulled right out of the mast and the lift line, block, and U-bolt connection went zinging off into the sky—with one end of the line still fastened to the staysail boom below. It zigged and zagged wildly in the wind and instantly got fouled in the shrouds. George and I were in the cockpit planning our line handling for a tack when this happened. We scrambled forward, and I, holding on to the shrouds, leaned out over the rushing water, grabbed the shackle holding the line to the little spar, and snapped it open, releasing the staysail. Wow, colorful and exciting!

I don't know if the lads were alarmed by this stuff. I hope not. They seemed to take it in stride, and it looked as if they were having as much fun as I was. Anyway, we just kept going.

The good news is that my double-sheet rig for the staysail boom actually worked pretty well. It took a couple of tries when we tacked to do a coordinated trimming job, with one of the lads on one side letting go while the other lad on the other side hauled in and secured his line. Also, the little boom pole really did clear the shrouds as it swung out, because when the wind filled the sail the boom was automatically lifted and had clearance.

This sail, I found out later, is really a self-tending staysail. It requires no sheets back to the cockpit. No hauling, trimming, tightening, winching, etc. The sail just goes left to right, right to left with the wind as you tack around. Cool. But on this day it was rigged as a little jib, with two sheets, one on either side of the mast, running back to the cockpit.

Our first tack went well except for the important fact that we had failed to tie down everything in the cabin before we left the dock. As we swung about and LILIBET took a deep lunge to starboard, there was a loud thud below; that was the stove crashing from one side of the boat to the other, along with packets of light bulbs, the engine manual, binoculars, a big yellow flashlight, a box of oil filters, odd cans, etc. Now I know why the cabin looked like it did when I first stepped aboard in Annapolis. Good thing, I reflected as I dashed down the now radically slanting steps to check for damage, that the stove wasn't connected to a gas line leading to a bottle somewhere. I could find no damage to my new cabinetry.

While things looked all messy down below, topsides we were clipping along at some unknown wonderful speed, heeled over with the deck rails just kissing the surface of the lake as it rushed by in a delightful gurgle. We tacked and sailed, and tacked and sailed. Sometimes we'd throw a little bow wave as we jammed along in the wind.

Since it was a Monday morning, there were almost no other boats on the lake. The wind continued to gain strength, but the sail wasn't crazy, just exhilarating. I had no speed instruments on board at the time, so I don't know how fast we were going, but it felt pretty fast. I remember the sight of the mast dipping toward the horizon and the lads sitting braced on the high side, and the feel of the wheel as I held LILIBET in that wonderful zone just off the wind so she slid along with her rail down. I sometimes got a little panicky, because there was that feeling that the boat would just lie down flat in the water, so I found myself steering her into the wind to ease the pressure on the sails so the boat would heel less. This, of course, also slowed her down; I found that I could ease her back off the wind a little, and she would lean over and speed up. What a feeling!

Frank spent most of his time in the cockpit with me, teaching me the finer points of sailing, which was a great help. While I had a very strong urge to climb all over the boat from stem to stern, observing every little thing about what was going on, I managed to stay and learn as much as I could. Mostly for this old stinkpotter, it was like riding a roller-coaster at the fun park for the first time. I hung on and tried to absorb as much as I could.

Everyone got a little nervous when it came time to jibe. Frank and George were of course very competent but had not seen yet how this big mainsail boom would handle, so they tried to prepare me for the eventuality of a severe head banging. A jibe is when you turn the stern of the boat through a following wind. It sometimes means the mainsail is out at a pretty big angle, perhaps even close to a right angle to the boat with the tail wind pushing you along forward billowing the sails out in front. This is sometimes called "surfing" and may be done with your headsail out to one side and your mainsail out to the other. This arrangement of sails is called "wing-and-wing." Now for some reason, maybe your running out of sea room, you decide to turn. To make this turn, you might bring the back of the boat through that following wind, thus putting that wind on the opposite side of the boat and this is called a jibe. You will also automatically be changing tacks, which means the wind, and sails will end up on the opposite side of the boat. I'll let you do your own research on port and starboard tacks, points of sail and all of that.

The only thing anyone cares about in a jibe is how to smoothly transfer that big mainsail full of wind from where it is now, back to where it points directly aft, then over to the opposite side, dumping wind as it comes while you are turning the rudder and the boat—of course after yelling like savages the time honored phrases "prepare to jibe" and "ready to jibe," answered by all crew members with "ready to jibe" or "no!" and the final savage yell when all hands respond correctly with "ready to jibe," is the phrase yelled at even a higher pitch "jibe ho." Then the helmsman begins his turn, and there wants to be no hesitation or showboating. The concept is to make a nice clean turn, with everybody ducking under the boom as it crosses the boat.

Now comes the fun part. Once the boom and sail come over the back of the boat, the sail will be empty of wind and you must continue the turn and the smooth swing of that sail and boom right across the stern of the boat and out to an appropriate angle perpendicular to this opposite side of the boat.

As the sail passes over the stern on its way around, it will appear like everything is just peachy. As the sail and boom pass across the wind however, the sail will want to fill again in a big dangerous blast of air that, without some control, will yank the whole rig around to the side with such force that it can break the mast, knock people down and cause all kinds of chaos. Uncontrolled, the boom will begin moving very fast once the turn is started and by the time it rounds the stern and the mainsail fills with wind, there really is no stopping it. So control is the watchword.

This is where something called the main sheet comes in. When I was a stinkpot driver, I thought that sheets on sailboats were the sails. Actually, sheets are lines, or ropes used to rig all the various sails on the boat. Collectively, these lines are called the running rigging. Some of them have special names like the main sheet, which is a slightly complicated, long length of stout cordage run through a series of blocks (pulleys) that make it possible to reduce the great force of wind through these pulleys so you can control the wild mainsail in its arc around the back end of your boat. One end of the main sheet is attached to the end of the boom, then the rope is led down through this block system, attached again to a metal slide called a traveler or car as you will, which goes from one side of the cockpit to the other, back of the steering station and allows for controlled movement of the boom and mainsail via the main sheet apparatus, across the width of the cockpit. The end of the main sheet runs off on a long length to be let out or taken in depending on the set of your sails as you move through the water.

The idea in a tack is to let the main sheet apparatus swing with the boom across the boat at the same time the helmsman makes his turn. As the boom swings around the main sheet is drawn in or let out as necessary, helping to control the boom and allowing the mainsail to be set in its new tack. In a jibe, the mainsheet must be gingerly drawn in as the boom swings to the center of the boat and then gingerly eased out as the boat comes about. The mainsheet is used to prevent the boom from slamming over to the other side of the boat and causing damage to rigging or crew. There's also a little lock on the main sheet that prevents things slipping away when the correct trim is reached. Once the boom crosses the stern of the boat in either a tack or a controlled jibe, and the wind gets into the mainsail again on the reverse side, you will ease the main sheet out letting the boom continue to swing out or draw it in until the mainsail is set as you like. All this should reach a peaceful climax as the helmsman completes his turn and the boat steadies on her new course. It should be pointed out that this maneuver will take perhaps 30 seconds most of the time and will in a good wind be accompanied by a sudden lunge of the boat when it reverses heel, tipping from one side to the other as the wind comes at her from the new angle.

Our jibing exercise went well enough except that none of us had thought to make sure the entire length of main sheet line stayed behind the helmsman (that was me), so when the boom crossed overhead and the line began to tighten up in a flurry of snake-like activity in the cockpit, I found myself momentarily lashed around the chest. This was bad. Frank instantly reached over and flung the rope off so no damage was done, but we all agreed to keep an eye on where that line should be next time we did a jibe and I remarked to myself that this whole sailing deal was going to take some concentrated practice. Since then I've noticed a lot of folks tend to rely on tacking as the preferred way to come about. I can see why. It's easier than jibing.

Re-setting the headsails is a whole other regimen in the coming about exercise. I'll just say that on my boat there are two jib sheets that lead from the bottom aft end of the head sail back past either side of the cabin and ending up wrapped around a port and a starboard winch. The winches are used to set the headsails on the desired tack or course and are alternated in their use depending on which side of the boat the wind is on. Sounds complicated but it's not.

Additionally, on my boat, we have a set of running backstays, which are port and starboard mast braces—sort of a cross between standing and running rigging, that go from just under the lower set of spreaders on the mast, aft and down to the port and starboard headsail winches. These running backstays help support the mast when it is under stress from the wind. They are tightened and loosened alternately as the boat goes from starboard to port tack. It's another job to be done in speedy order back there in the cockpit. I learned all this while sailing with my pals one windy, sunny day on Lake Minnetonka.

We angled our way down the lake to Wayzata Bay, at the far end of the lake from our home port. There's a new restaurant in the town of Wayzata, right on the water, and Frank knew the owner. I knew it would be fun to sail in and tie up for lunch. Frank was thinking the same, but the wind was kicking up pretty strong by now. We talked about it as we searched for the channel going in. Checking lake charts I had purchased from our local boat supply store, we found slightly less detail than we could wish for, especially at this time of year when the lake level had dropped about two feet from normal. I was especially nervous about threading channels in and out of tight places without a depthfinder. In some ways, not having a depthfinder was probably better, because I'm sure we were very close to the bottom and seeing it on a screen would only have given me a heart attack and ruined the fun.

The knowledge that the lake bottom in Wayzata Bay is fairly silty, without a lot of big submerged objects—except for the occasional car that drops through the ice in early and late winter—made us more daring than perhaps was prudent, and we sailed on. Our chart showed two long bars coming from the shore on both sides of the channel. There should have been a hazard marker for each of those bars, but one marker was missing. We weren't sure which bar the remaining marker belonged to so we guessed, and, of course, it was a wrong guess.

When we touched bottom there was a fairly definite hesitation in our forward motion, but no big jarring, grinding, shuddering halt. With the wind blowing as it was, we had a fair amount of forward momentum, and the sails stayed full as we forged across the bar. We could feel the rasping drag of keel on bottom. No one made a sound as we held our breath for ten seconds, and when we cleared the bottom everyone happily acted as though this was a normal happening. Maybe it was.

We entered the bay, which when seen from land seems plenty large enough for a sailboat to cruise around in with room to spare. As it turned out, it was a challenge just tacking around in the confined space, because we never really thought about reefing (shortening the sails) or, better yet, simply dropping our sails. In hindsight, it may have been better to drop our sails and motor in once we cleared the bar, so we could putt around the bay and feel cool.

As we moved closer and closer to what I knew to be a shallow shoreline, Frank would precede every turn by saying, "Okay guys, let's talk about this." Which was terrific, because he was teaching me stuff by doing this. It was wonderfully exciting and a little scary. What if we ended up beached in the middle of this ritzy little Midwestern town? I could hear the town crowd yelling down from the sidewalks above, "We told you that sailboat was too big for our lake!" Well, of course that didn't happen, but this end of the lake was getting the most wind of the day. It seemed magnified here.

Much as we liked the idea of running in to the guest dock by the restaurant and taking our ease at the nice umbrella tables along the waterfront, I think we were all glad when we agreed to get back out on the open lake. George busied himself with the staysail, which was performing beautifully even though we all knew it still wasn't rigged exactly right. Frank and I tried to figure out how to get out on the big lake again by a different route, and succeeded in not touching bottom this time.

By early afternoon, we dropped the sails and motored into the Shorewood Yacht Club marina. By now I had a pretty good feel for coming into the moorage; the wind on this end was pretty light, so it was easy. I checked the bilge and was only slightly surprised to see a large amount of water above the standard level. Of course, LILIBET had been heeled over on her side most of the day, and those black topsides hadn't been submerged in at least three years. As tight as the planking appeared to be, it was clear that the seams were dried out enough to allow the entry of lots of water—and then, of course, there is always the matter of movement in a wooden hull when it's put under stress. I won't know how much movement there would be in LILIBET till I sailed her more. I pumped her out and joined the lads for a crab-and-scallop salad back in that restaurant in Wayzata we almost visited by boat earlier in the day.

This was the second to the last official day of summer. The next day it rained and the rest of the week was not that great, either, so actually, this was my one real day of sailing on LILIBET for the year. I was sad Georgia hadn't been with us, and so was she, but we both knew there would be sailing days again, if not this fall, then next spring. Evening conversations around the dinner table had us discovering our two-year project was coming to an end. We were feeling quite ready to let the season come to a close so we could look forward to a winter of something other than the boat. It was time.

The rest of September and the first half of October flashed past. At this time last year, we were on the riverbank in St. Paul caulking the decks. Now, even though there were a handful of perfect sailing days left in the month, it was clear the season in Minnesota was over. My daily visits to the marina after work revealed little activity on the docks, and as the days went by, I noticed the yard boys had begun to haul boats out of the lake. One nice afternoon I discovered my neighbor missing and spotted the blue fiberglass hull up by the tree line on a cradle.

Speaking of cradles, back in August I decided to build one for LILIBET rather than pay another outrageous yard fee to have one provided. I got the usual raised-eyebrow response from folks I know, but went right ahead figuring out how to build a collapsible steel boat cradle that would hold up the great yacht LILIBET and not fall over in a wind.

On a warm Sunday morning, Georgia and I drove over to the old marina in St. Paul and searched around until we found the cradle we had used for the past two years. It was stashed out in a weed field with thirty or forty others plus the remains of a couple of old wooden boat hulls that had been cut up for firewood. I measured all the lengths and heights of the metal boat stand and wrote them down. For the next six weeks, I made an occasional stop at the steel yards over in the industrial part of town on my way to work and loaded up pieces of long, square metal stock tubing. I dropped these off at the sculpture studio at the art center before I hit the office, and throughout the days that followed, whenever things got slow, I used the welding equipment to construct six oversized angle jacks with adjustable heights and bottom connector sections so I could bolt these together and make a good fit to the boat when we craned her out. I bought some old, round, tube-type stands from a woman whose husband had sold his boat, and converted the screw tops to fit my cradle. By October 15, the cradle was ready to go.

John, the marina owner who likes to worry about everything at his boatyard, started making lots of fishy references to "that cradle thing that you're making." I almost started worrying myself. Just to make everyone feel better, I spray-painted it hunter green. I delivered the cradle about a week before we hauled out, and everyone's eyes got big. Finally one of the yard boys said in passing, "That there's some slick cradle, man." This made me feel good.

On a blustery evening in the third week of October, I

met John at the yard after work to schedule a crane for the haulout. He had freaked out about the size of the Rocket crane rig last spring and had gone into paralysis about the cost and the impact the big crane had on his parking lot. He found another outfit, and we were there to meet the new guys. They were tough-looking heavy-machinery operators with dirty duds and faces. I got visions of my old marina experience in St. Paul and started to get a headache. John was watching to see if I was going to be a jerk and make demands, but I didn't. They had never lifted a boat before, and I was plenty squeamish but figured this was just another set of boat problems on inland waters. Cold weather would probably be right on schedule, and I didn't want to have to chop ice from around LILIBET's hull because I didn't trust some crane guys. They measured the boat and listened to my instructions about straps and spreaders and placement of the straps along the hull. There really isn't that much involved when it comes to lifting a boat out and in, especially once you've done it, but all boat owners still get nervous anyway. We settled on a price and a date.

A week later I slid out of work around 11 a.m. and drove over to the marina. The crane was just getting set up, so I went down to the boat and started up the engine. One of the marina lads climbed aboard to help handle lines, and we slid out into the pond. It was a rainy, gray, cold day, and I rather enjoyed the end-of-season feel of things. I crimped her around and putted into the lift slot just as it was supposed to be done. We stopped and never touched the concrete ramp. I shut off Mr. Perkins and stepped off feeling pretty smart. The crane came around and we slipped the big yellow slings under the rudder and forward along the keel to the lifting points on the hull I now pretty much knew by heart. A few minutes later the crane gave a power grunt and slowly lifted LILIBET from the water—up and around and over the docks and parking lot to where we were busily assembling my slick new boat cradle. It was a little tricky because of the uneven ground and gravel base in the lot, but within 15 minutes we had the cradle ready and the crane lowered LILIBET onto the built-up beams at the base of the cradle that would support her all winter.

Well, it was a little trickier than that. You know, the right angles and the leveling of the deck and the plumb of the mast and the shims under the keel. Oh, and of course, there were plenty of experts standing around, but I welcomed their eyes. There's a wonderful kind of camaraderie that happens when a nice old wooden girl like LILIBET gets moved about. Even a few of my dock neighbors were on hand to snap pictures.

Finally, LILIBET was snugged in tightly for the winter, and I climbed aboard to close her up. A week later, Georgia and I spent a sunny Saturday custom-fitting plastic tarps over her so she'd stay dry during the winter snows and blows. I must say, we were getting pretty good at this. The lads pumped some antifreeze through Mr. Perkins, and I took note of the hull, seeing the need for some good caulking work next spring before we put her back in. I'll read up on that again, over the months ahead.

Now it's December '04. The light fails around 4:30 p.m. this time of year in the inland sea country. Georgia and I are enjoying our rest from the last two years of bringing that yacht LILIBET along. I think my biggest fear was of getting behind in the project and ending up with this big old unfinished hulk and lots of "I told you so's." Thankfully that didn't happen, and we both, with much bending to the task, learned a lot. I highly recommend it. From here forward, it will be a steady maintenance issue, of course—and there's a summer ahead of learning to sail. We'll take pictures.

EPILOG

In late March of that year, I redid the bottom while LILIBET was standing in my nifty green cradle with her nose pointing out to the lake. This time I scoured out lots of old dried-up caulking (not the cotton) and replaced it with black goo from a boat-store tube. It's good stuff and worked great. The process was toilsome as usual, and my fiberglass fellows at the marina were surprised at both the amount of work and the resilience of that old guy with the wooden boat. A couple of them even got into redoing the paint on their own boats, and for a week or two I wasn't the only one walking around looking like a chimney sweep.

When we dropped her in around April 1, there was very little water intake, and I felt both relieved and pleased with my work. After a couple of grinds, the diesel started up and quickly smoothed out to a civilized rumble as I backed the boat out of the launch slot and rounded for our slip at the end of the pier. It was a beautiful, sunny day, and I had a dock neighbor on board and one on the pier to help handle the tie-up part. Everything went fine.

Georgia and I were determined to learn how to sail this boat, so we rigged the mainsail in its slides and fastened the staysail to its little boom on the first weekend after launch. We greased the mast and boom slides, and raised the mainsail at the dock—first checking that there was no wind to knock us about at the dock. It went up smoothly and came down just as well. Our neighbors were encouraging, but not exactly stepping forward to join us at sea, so we untied the lines and backed LILIBET out into the pond. Thrilling. As we cleared the channel, the breeze picked up just a trifle, and we cruised toward the first of several bays that make up our route to the main part of the lake. This is where one typically raises the sails, cuts the engine, and slides out into the lake. Georgia and I talked about it, and being cautious in our early spring ways—sort of like the bears poking their noses out of the den after waking from the winter slumber—we said, " Let's just get used to this thing again before we take the plunge." We cruised around for awhile, checked things here and there, listened to Mr. Perkins, and headed back to the marina.

The following week we were back on the boat, and this time while Georgia held LILIBET to the wind, I cranked up the mainsail and then the staysail—which by now we had correctly decided was indeed a self-tending sail and in between tacks, tends to flop back and forth while deciding where it wants to be. Once the sails were up, I killed the engine and things got quiet as we heeled over slightly and headed up the bay-way toward the lake. Looking over the stern, we could see a tidy little wake as LILIBET slid forward.

"Okay, here's what we know," we said. If you point directly at the wind, the boat will stop. That's the scientific truth, so don't point directly into the wind—unless you have a need to come to a stop out there in the lake. Then it's okay, but you'll have to get going again by bringing her off the wind a little. If you can't shift your sails around to catch some wind and get going, use Mr. Perkins. This boat is narrow, with big sails and a heavy keel, so she can sail pretty close to the wind—meaning that if the wind is coming from 12 o'clock, you can just about point at 11 or 1 o'clock if there's a fair wind, and she'll move forward. I know now that, with a 15- to 20-mph breeze, LILIBET will lie over with her rail on the water and skid along right quick when she is close to the wind. It's fun. In a more than 20-mph wind things can get downright exciting.

The other big truth we knew is that you don't change wind direction from one side of the boat to the other (that would be tacking and jibing) without proper planning, and of course shouting all the traditional jargon. Okay, these things we know. By now the boat was reaching midway into the open bay-way, and we were feeling pretty fine. But there must be more we should know.

There is. Points of sail are good to know. Briefly, for those who have never heard of this stuff, points of sail are just wind directions and the set of your sails in relation to those directions. If the wind is blowing toward you from aft, over your right shoulder as you face forward, you could be said to be running with the wind and your point of sail might be what is called a run, or a reach, or a beam reach, or even perhaps a broad reach, meaning your sails are out to the right or starboard side of the boat filled with wind coming from behind or slightly behind (at your right shoulder as you face the bow of the boat).

Likewise, if the wind is coming at you from anywhere forward of the middle of the hull—as you face the bow on let's say the starboard side—you would pull the sails in so they can act like an airfoil and cause forward motion. This is called beating, and the closer you steer into that wind, the closer you draw in the sails (this is called sailing to weather, and it's really fun most of the time)—until of course, you've steered too close to the wind, like directly at it, and the sails start to flap and flutter as they empty while you drift to a stop. Don't do that.

There's a million fine points to this discussion, all of which come clear with practice and none of which we knew much about on this fine morning, so we just puffed along learning as we went.

Because the breeze was indeed coming mildly from our aft starboard quarter, over our right shoulders, and we finally recognized the need to make a turn because we were going toward shore, we knew that in this turn we could bring the nose of the boat through the wind in a tack. We also could bring the stern of the boat through the wind in a jibe. That would be a turn to the left, and for complex reasons, of the two choices, it is the turning maneuver entailing the greatest risk and the most careful execution. Which one do you guess we did? While we didn't exactly savagely yell out the time-honored commands regarding the jibe (since we were standing next to each other), we did say them out loud—"prepare to jibe" "ready to jibe?" "jibe ho!"—and it was pretty cool.

Georgia made the turn, smoothly bringing the bow to the left and swinging the stern to the right through the following wind. As she did, the big mainsail boom started its swing toward the center of the boat. I was stationed just behind the boom crutch and had the main sheet well in hand. As the boom swung toward me I reeled in the loose sheet, snugging the boom against a free flight across the boat and out to the other side. As Georgia completed the turn, I eased the mainsheet out so the sail could find a temporary place to be while we adjusted the running backstays. All went well in our very first sailing maneuver. What a treat.

We tried the jibe a couple of more times and experienced at least one slammer—how it happened, I don't know, but nothing was damaged because the air was so light, and we were in jibe mode anyway, so it wasn't a big surprise. Still, like many folks before us, we think the preferred turn will be a tack.

After a couple of hours, the wind dropped to almost nothing, and we became becalmed as we headed home. Finally, we fired up the diesel and motored to the dock. While the whole thing was small change compared to the sea adventures lining my bookshelves at home, the day was a terrific learning exercise for us, and we felt super.

Later that night, I started thinking that it was now time to enjoy the boat and that we should find a good crew to go sailing with us so Georgia and I could really get this down.

I pondered the possibilities for a week or two. Lots of

lads at the marina had said they'd like to go out on the boat, but none had really suggested participating in a season of sailing. Some were probably put off by our inexperience, and our brashness in thinking we could master the task of handling the big boat. I don't blame them. Some, in the Minnesota way, didn't want to impose. Most just had too many other things on their plate.

I thought about posting a "crew wanted" note on the club bulletin board, but honestly, I wasn't confident in my sailboat handling or skippering skills and, like most guys, didn't want to prove my foolishness to people I had to share the parking lot with. Frank and George were off doing their own stuff, and so for a minute there I was stumped. Then I remembered a conversation with Marliss, the sculptor's wife, in which she mentioned that her son Maury and his girlfriend Becky were avid and capable sailors. It had been a long time since we had seen Marliss and Steve—almost a year, when we had invited them to spend an afternoon on the dock during the yacht club commodore's races just at the time when our engine was still dead and we had to hang out. The day came out great, and they got to experience the decidedly relaxed atmosphere of this little yacht club. We just couldn't sail, and the idea struck me that it might be a good thing to call them up.

As it turned out, Maury and Becky had completed the sailing courses offered on the lake, and owned a seventeen-or-so-foot-long daysailer, which they trailered to one of the in-city park lakes. They were both good at sail and line handling, and Becky proved to be an excellent helmswoman. Steve and Marliss came, too—everyone dressed in wonderfully sporty boating attire. I believe this was Father's day, and as I watched Steve and Maury together on the boat, I admired their ability to be together pretty much whenever they liked. I also experienced a little pang of sadness thinking of my own son and my father, both living in Florida and quite out of reach on fun days like this.

I walked everyone through what I knew about the boat and what I did not know about sailing. Maury and Becky pitched right in, exploring the boat, examining the rigging, getting familiar with where things were and how they worked, and letting their feet get used to the deck layout. Steve and I followed along and added our two-cents' worth when we had a chance. Finally, I cranked up the engine and got behind the helm. Everyone else lined the deck and unfastened the sail covers. It was the first time I got to see an actual crew working together on LILIBET's decks, and it was pretty nifty. We untied and slid out of the moorage, made our turn, and powered out into the bay. For our first crewed sailing session, there wasn't a lot of wind, but we did go sailing and everyone got to see how she handled.

From that time on, we took the boat out almost every weekend. Those rust-colored sails became a familiar sight out on the lake, and we got lots of compliments from other boaters. Once, as we sailed up the bay-way toward the open lake, an antique World War II fighter plane on his way to an air show somewhere nearby spotted LILIBET on the water and swooped down for a closer look. As he flew past he blew a long line of smoke out of an exhaust port and waggled his wings.

During the summer of weekend sailing, everyone took

Georgia at the helm in a nice stiff wind while Jack hauls the main sheet, Lake Minnetonka, Summer 2005

a turn at the wheel, except Marliss, who specialized in enjoying the ride and providing great company and delicious lunches. We learned that while LILIBET enjoys sailing to weather—or better said perhaps, we enjoy sailing to weather—it can be quite a physical workout. With a good, strong wind blowing in on the forward quarter, you haul in the sails close to the center of the boat and hold on tight. Don't forget to close the porthole covers. We tried out a few different sail combinations, including our big white genoa sail, which really worked well. The crew worked wonderfully together, and even the skipper remained calm enough while we all learned to operate this grand old sailboat.

It's now the end of this second summer on the lake, and haulout time is close at hand. I'm feeling very satisfied with this project and of course am wondering about the future of my pretty boat. I'm hoping for one more season on the lake so Georgia and I can get truly comfortable handling LILIBET as a duo. Then, who knows? Bigger water will eventually call and there's always a good chance that it won't be me at the helm. The sale of one's boat is always an eventual consideration, and I wonder if some new restoration project is on the horizon. I also wonder if any future project could give me as much enjoyment as this one has. Time has a way of letting one know of course, but I'm certainly not in a rush.

Appendix

LILIBET's history and technical data

LILIBET was designed by Norman Edward Dallimore and built in 1937.

LILIBET is a cutter rigged sloop. She is 42' on deck and 36' at the waterline. She is 9' wide at the beam. She weighs 24,000 lbs - 12 tons. She is built of pitch pine planking over oak frames. Her decks are teak, sprung planked. She is fastened with copper rivets. She has a 4-ton lead keel. She has a 4-cylinder Perkins diesel engine.

Her mast is 55' tall Sitka spruce, and steps on the keel forward of midships. She has a full galley and a stand-up head. She sleep 2 comfortably in the forward compartment and 2 more uncomfortably in quarterberths on either side of the cockpit. She has a mainsail, self-tending staysail, a storm jib, a genoa ¾, a spinaker and a cruising jib.

Norman Edward Dallimore
(1883-1959)

Yacht Designer and Surveyor

Norman Edward Dallimore grew up in London, and started sailing in his early teens.

In 1908 he was part owner of DOROTHY, a 27-foot gaff cutter, and it was in that year that he drew his first design. She was an 8-ton sloop and the first of many designs that he entered in *Yachting Monthly* competitions.

In 1910 he owned AIRLIE, also a 27-foot gaff cutter, which he raced in the three years 1911-1913. He won the cup in each of these consecutive years.

During the 1914–18 war he served as an R.N.V.R. Lieutenant in Motor Launches. Then he became a fire insurance surveyor with The Royal Exchange Assurance for a number of years, and designed boats at night.

From 1921 onwards he formed a close but unofficial partnership with William King & Sons of Burnham who built 22 of his designs.

A few of his designs were motor cruisers, all of which had one characteristic in common, the hint of a clipper bow.

Among the well-known boats he designed were:

1927   DAFFODIL for Percy Sable. She was the first Bermudan rigged staysail schooner to be built in the UK.

1934   LEILA for "Pills" Holloway.

1937   PHYNELLA for Frank and Horace Pitcher. She had a moveable bulkhead to suit different requirements down below.

1937   BLUE TROUT for Jimmy Smart. The largest sailing boat to have been built in Burnham. Town Cup winner in 1938 with Dallimore at the helm.

1937   LILIBET for Major Bill Noot

During his 45-year career as a designer he produced 184 designs of which 58 were built. He had an artistic eye so that most of his boats were pretty, having a curved stem, a counter stern and, in between, a proper sheer. He also drew 191 sail plan conversions and hull modifications, and there was also a steady demand for his expertise as a yacht surveyor.

He was a gifted helmsman who had an instinctive feel for a boat. He particularly enjoyed sailing in heavy weather.

He would have been very pleased to find so many of his boats in commission today, but he probably would not have been surprised because not only was he careful to ensure that his specifications were right, but also because he knew that the workmanship in the yards where the boats were built, and the materials used, were of very high quality.

Lines drawing of LILIBET

Alternate Plans for 12-tonner
Lilibet in April 1937

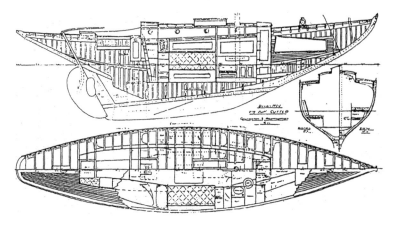

The lay-out of Major Noot's boat embodies a two-berth cabin forward.

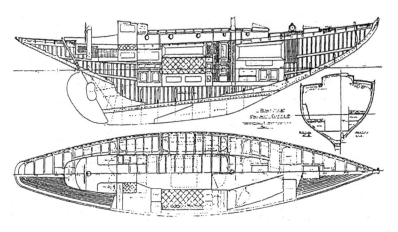

Mr. C. G. Yickers' boat has a fo'c'sle and a passage berth aft.